No Words, Only Tears

My Journey through Depression

DIANE SUMMERS

ISBN 978-1-64492-651-2 (paperback)
ISBN 978-1-64492-652-9 (digital)

Christian Faith Publishing, Inc.
832 Park Avenue
Meadville, PA 16335
www.christianfaithpublishing.com

Printed in the United States of America

I have tried to recreate events, conversations, and locales from my memories of them. In some instances, names as well as identifying characteristics of some individuals have been changed to maintain their anonymity.

CONTENTS

Part 2 — Searching for Sanity

Part 3 — Anecdotes of Darkness

Part 4 — Rebirth

I dedicate this book to my husband Murray and my sons
Paul and Jeff—their love made this book possible.

ACKNOWLEDGMENTS

To my family, who have traveled with me on this traumatic and chaotic journey and who have stood by me through the darkness of my troubled life, I thank you.

To my husband Murray, for his unwavering love and support, who painstakingly typed and retyped this manuscript until it passed my critical inspection. I love and thank you.

My eternal gratitude goes out to my sons, Paul and Jeff for their patience, acceptance and love. I ask for your forgiveness for the wounds that I've passed on to you.

To my friend Laureen Foster, thank you for your support and encouragement during the early stage of my writing when I first decided to change a short presentation into a book.

To my friend Ida Rawluk, for her moral support and upbeat attitude, who patiently checked quotes and references and Googled answers to my endless questions throughout the writing process. You are my favourite "research assistant."

To my brother Ralph Mask, whose artistic talent inspired the book cover and captured the essence of that first dark farmhouse which insinuated itself into my reality during the earliest and most formative years of my childhood.

To my sister-in-law Joyce Mask, who was most helpful, a special thank you for her patience, dedication and insight. I thank her from the bottom of my heart for her endless hours of work in bringing this book together. Without her expertise, it would have been extremely difficult for me to complete the editorial stage and achieve my goal of completing this book.

To my sister Marie Lacombe who, in addition to her in-depth historical knowledge, provided love and support, and words of wisdom that kept me moving forward and on the right track.

Last but not least, I must acknowledge my deepest gratitude to God who ultimately gave me the strength to transform my tears into words, and the courage to turn those words into this story of my life, which I hope will help others find their words.

No matter how bad your mother and father may have been,
some day you have to stand by their graveside
and recognize what they gave you,
forgive what they did to you and receive the
spirit that is in your life because of them.
Ron Rolheiser, OMI

PART

1

Genesis

Why Am I Afraid to Tell You Who I Am?

They say that you really don't know a person until you have walked a mile in their shoes. I would like to go a step further and say; "You really don't know a person until you have felt the pain of their tears."

I have always been a very private person. I am the person who, long ago, came across the book titled *Why Am I Afraid to Tell You Who I Am?* by John Powell S.J. and I said to myself, "This is me." So deciding to put words to what lies in my heart and sharing them is very unlike me. And I know that, once I put this out there, I can never take back these words—these words that come from deep within me and are deeply personal, words that might not even be accepted. But yet something in me says "It's time." I feel so very vulnerable and scared. But if I can help just one person persevere when they feel that their life is in chaos and that they are falling into that deep, dark pit of despair, it will have been worth all the soul searching I have done to write this, and all the pain so many of the memories have brought. And yet, for every word that I have written, there are a thousand words I have left unsaid—words that I still cannot bring myself to write.

Everyone has a life story to tell because *every* soul's journey back to God is unique. This is my story, the way I remember it, the way I felt it, and the way I lived it.

I am the fourth oldest in my family. My childhood recollections are not those of happy birthdays, Merry Christmases or fuzzy bonding during family outings. My earliest memory is of myself at the age of three. I am sliding down the unfinished wooden stairs on my bum, and in my arms, I am carrying my newborn baby sister. While other three-year-olds might be sitting on a parent's lap listening to nursery rhymes or being sung to, I was being a mother. And this was just the beginning. Four brothers, another sister, a stillborn brother, and my mother's two miscarriages followed.

To say that life was hard would be a gross understatement; it would be laughable. But there was little time or reason to laugh, especially during those early years.

I was raised on a farm in unnecessary poverty and isolation. It was not a farm in the true sense of the word because it was not our livelihood. We had some cows for milk, pigs to slaughter, and my father's hunting hounds—dogs that meant more to him than his children.

We had no electricity which meant, no fridge, no electric stove or wash machine and no dryer. We had no luxuries like a plug-in radio, a toaster, or an electric kettle. We had no central heating, no indoor plumbing, and none of the comforts that come with running water. Microwaves, disposable diapers and baby bottles were things of the future.

We had nothing. This was not an episode from *Survivor*; this was our reality.

The Wonder Years

> I know what I really want for Christmas. I
> want my childhood back. Nobody is going
> to give me that. I know it doesn't make sense,
> but since when is Christmas about sense,
> anyway? It is about a child, of long ago and
> far away, and it is about the child of now. In
> you and me. Waiting behind the door of our
> hearts for something wonderful to happen.
> —Robert Fulghum

I write at length about childhood because that's where our life stories all begin.

This is my life story and it's the only story I'm qualified to write. Read it with your heart because that is where I live and where I write from. So much of what I say has been said before—but not by me. So I feel compelled to put it into words that say it my way.

I struggle with these words in my effort to describe not only the events that happened, but also how they impacted me—and how I have dealt with them. My ultimate goal is to "show" readers what the inside of a depressed person's mind looks and feels like—the what and the how of what they are trying to process as they struggle to live with this insidious disease called depression.

The healthy development of a child depends on being loved and accepted unconditionally, at least in the beginning. Children learn to love by being loved. They need to see love mirrored to them. They need to feel that they matter.

Our childhood shapes us individually; it forms us. Uniquely, it programs us. We carry its remnants within us for the rest of our lives. What we are today is a result of its influences—the good and the bad. And we often have the challenging task of dealing with our childhood—our upbringing—of examining it and deciding what to keep and what to discard.

I was never a child, not in the sense that almost anyone would define a child. Being raised in an extremely dysfunctional family, I never lived those carefree, innocent wonder years by which a normal childhood is characterized. And a lost childhood is hard to recover—to reclaim. It takes an enormous amount of time and work, effort and energy, and can be extremely painful. But coming to terms with it can be done. Of that, I am living proof. Yes, for years—for decades—I was part of the walking wounded: angry, sad, lonely, fearful, anxious, distrustful, hateful, hopeless—that is, clinically depressed. Feelings ruled my life; depression ruled my life. The lack of essential childhood developmental foundation left me with life-damaging consequences. For so many years, I was merely a shell, an empty casing of the person God meant me to be.

Those "wonder years," about which the poet Wordsworth wrote just never lived in me!

My Mother

I have a picture of my Mom and Dad holding my oldest brother's hands as he stands between them. He was a toddler around the age of one. They look so normal, even happy. They look like any other couple with their first child. Mom looks proud and stylish, beautiful. But that was before my father moved his young family to isolation and to a life of deprivation. That fateful move set the stage for the rest of our lives. My mother was not strong enough to stand up for her needs or those of her growing family. My father was not someone with whom you could bargain. He was the boss. She followed where he led and became the victim of circumstances which today we call domestic violence. I wonder what happens to broken hearts, to shattered dreams? Where do they go? Where did my mother's go? Did my Dad ever have any?

My parents may have loved each other in the beginning, but they never said, "I love you," to each other or to us kids. And it wasn't something that was taken for granted in our family; the feeling was just never there. Ten siblings all messed up because no one learned to say, "I love you," and you cannot begin to truly live until you learn to love. And you cannot truly love another until you learn to love yourself. This is the truth I was to discover during my years of searching for happiness, for love.

I remember my mother as a cold, passive, submissive woman, chronically tired and understandably so under the circumstances. In an age when disposable baby bottles and diapers were unheard of, she had four children under the age of five to cope with, in third-world living conditions. With no running water, central heating, electric lights, or appliances, she did what she had to do to keep us alive. But there was no time for nurturing, no time for bonding. Love was not spoken of. It was difficult enough to provide for the physical needs of four small children. The mental and emotional needs weren't even recognized, and the spiritual needs, well they were questionable. It was a meager existence.

Over the next fourteen years six more siblings rounded out the family, but by then, there were those of us old enough to help out and do chores. This was the way people lived in those days—so I'm told. Siblings helped raise siblings. In later years, we tended to say we weren't raised; we were dragged up, or worse still, we dragged each other up.

My mother's life was a hard and thankless struggle. There were no neighbors close enough for a coffee break or even a weekly visit. It wouldn't have mattered anyway, there was no time. And besides, my mother was not inclined that way. In the early years, especially, she was what might have been described as an over worked, stressed out, impatient caretaker, in a group home of angry and sometimes volatile delinquents—a situation that can escalate quickly when there is no meaningful discipline or role modeling or love in a home. There was very little happiness or joy in Mom's lonely life and very little to look forward to. She was what, in today's terms, would be called *depressed*, but that was not a condition or an illness, not even a word that was recognized or used back then. For most of my life I too lived with the tiredness and apathy, the anxiety and anger that chronic depression inflicts. So in spite of her shortcomings as a person and as a mother, looking back, I understand and sympathize with her and her situation.

Unfortunately my mother also had a mean streak, as was evident when she gave my youngest sister, merely a child, a pail of water and told her to teach the kittens how to swim. I did not fall victim to such cruelty as often as some of my siblings, perhaps because I was always trying to be helpful. But her remarks could be caustic, and even now, I cringe as I vividly remember her words. As time passed, she developed passive-aggressive tendencies and became manipulative.

It wasn't until my teen years that I had any real relationship with my mother. It was only then that she became more of a person to me and less of a bossy, judgemental authority figure. There were some precious moments of laughter, such as when we made "hermit" cookies and they turned out rock-hard. We reasoned that, perhaps, that was why they were called hermits—they had to live alone, because their unyielding texture meant no one wanted to have anything to do with them—a rare foolish moment. Our radio station would begin the morning program at five a.m. with an instrumental violin tune called, "Maple Sugar." Mom really enjoyed it, as four of her brothers were violin players. Sometimes we would get up early just to listen to this tune. That was one of a few things I do remember sharing. When the song was over she would go back to bed, but I'd stay up and enjoy the early morning calm and stillness before I had to wake up the rest of the kids and the noise began.

Mom never graduated from high school, yet she had the most beautiful penmanship. I'm not sure why or how, but I still have some of her cards and letters, and even some of her handwritten recipes. To me, they're like a glimpse of another person, perhaps that woman who looked so nice when she had time to curl her hair and put on makeup—rouge and lipstick—before going to church on Sunday morning.

For some reason, I loved bright colors. Perhaps they reminded me of my beloved autumn leaves. In any case, I bought a remnant of bright-orange material, and without questioning her creativity or doubting her sewing ability, I asked Mom to make me a dress. There was just barely enough material, and without so much as a pattern, she sewed a sleeveless V-neck sundress with an encased tie around the waist. She had talent; if only life had not been so cruel and squashed it. If only…if only…

As the years went by her passive-aggressive personality became more manipulative and controlling. By this time in our lives my youngest brother and sister were seven and eight years old, so Mom's time was more her own. The daily routine of diapers and bottles was past. But some things never change. In these later years, when her life could have been so much better, the apathy and resignation into which she had sank could not be reversed. It was too late for any significant change. It just didn't matter to her anymore.

Years later I am at my mother's funeral with all six of my brothers and my three sisters. We talk and reminisce, and some tears are shed. I feel very detached, removed from it all. I am there, but I am not really there. It is as if I do not connect to the present reality. My feelings are frozen. I kiss my mother goodbye, but I do not cry, not now, not yet.

I remember standing on the steps of the church. My husband gently turns me to face the funeral procession because I am looking elsewhere. It's as though I am lost in time—a time gone by—lost with a woman whose life was hard and lonely and plagued by depression. A woman, my mother, who could not give me what I needed because she had nothing to give.

It is months later. I am washing my kitchen floor and thinking, trying to make sense of the sheer tragedy of lives half lived—our lives, my mother's and mine—robbed of so much time and joy by depression. Like so many of my reactions—long delayed, the tears start, and I cry and cry.

I am finally grieving the death of my mother.

My Father

My father was a mechanic and a good one. It wasn't intelligence that he lacked. What he lacked was a decent sense of priorities, of family responsibilities, and of morality. Thankfully, God was merciful. My father's adulterous indiscretions were unbeknownst to me as I was growing up. Perhaps God, knowing my extremely sensitive nature, saw fit to hide them from me—to spare me that added shame. I was already dealing with more than I could handle.

I remember the Friday nights, in my early years, when my father would come home from work, on snowshoes, with his packsack on his back. In it would be his case of beer for the weekend and our groceries for the week. In the summer, the only thing that changed in this scenario was the weather. On the rare occasion that he took us anywhere, he'd stop at every beer parlor, accessible only to men in those days, and the rest of us would sit in the car, in the heat, and wait and wait. Milk could curdle in babies' bottles or run out altogether. And while there was money for the beer parlor stops, I have no recollections of ever going to a restaurant or having enough money for a pop. Later in life, I dubbed him "a weekend alcoholic."

Dad made good money and yet we lived in poverty. During the week, he had room and board in the place where he worked. He had three good meals a day, a warm bed, and no outside family responsibilities. He had a good life of sorts. We had a mere existence. At one point, he even had another woman who he visited along his way to and from work—very convenient, very callous, very heartbreaking. Even when he came home, he got his first choice—the one warm bedroom in the house. He had no qualms about his lifestyle.

To me, my father was the old man who came to our house and ranted and raved about what we kids had done or the chores that we had not done. Before he came home, I would examine my conscience to see if there was anything I had done that was especially bad, and if I thought there might be something, I was even more fearful. My father had a habit of persistently harassing the kids, especially my brothers. He could not stand to see them—as he called it—"doing nothing." He would bark out all of these orders. "Do this, do that, you didn't do that? Why not? Why not? What's wrong with you?" And then, more often than not, he would sit and do nothing. The impact of these verbal assaults on our very persons is hard to fathom, let alone describe. They cut to our very core and evoked feelings of fear, confusion, and yes, even hate. It was a tragedy that grew greater day by day.

His preferred method of discipline was his razor strap. It was used for more than sharpening his razor. As best I can remember, the girls were spared from this treatment, and yet I feared it. One of my younger brothers was especially defiant. The more our father strapped him, the more he rebelled. It was not a matter of a child being disciplined; it was a power struggle, and my brother would not give in. He would not be defeated. He was strapped a lot. I believe by the time he left home he was ready to kill our father.

For me, my father's presence was a source of angst that added to the chaos that I felt was our lives. As much as I could, I tried to avoid him. No real conversation ever took place between us. And I never wanted one. I knew he was my Dad, but he was also that stranger who lived in our house. And yet, in that sense, he fit in. We were all strangers to each other. Together but always apart.

There was no sense of peace when he was around. As a child, I feared him, and in my mind, as I grew older, I blamed him for everything that was wrong with our lives and our way of living. Gradually the fear turned into hate, a deep, long-lasting hate—hate for my father, the enemy, that despicable human who helped raise us in ways that scarred me and my siblings for life.

Then the concept of sin was introduced to my young conscience. "Honor your father and mother." I was guilty; I was a sinner. Yet another secret to add to the pain in my heart. I was merely a child.

I only remember defying him once. I can't recall the cause, but I do remember the consequences. He chased me and I ran around the heater stove, and as I went by the wood pile, I picked up a piece of wood and raised it. We were in a stand-off with the stove between us. He backed down and I was spared the wrath of his hand. My inner child remembers—too much for a child to forget.

My father seemed incapable of any lasting, happy emotions, and it seemed as if he needed to deny any happiness to his family as well. His was a conscience that had no trouble denying his family even the basic needs of sufficient food and decent shelter.

Even as a child, I could not reconcile my fathers' actions. He was that person who expected us to go to mass on Sundays, led the rosary in Polish during my younger years, and made me kneel with my siblings listening to words I didn't understand. Then he was that person who would drink away the grocery money when we were nearly starving. Groceries were not a priority with him—his beer, his dogs, and even his cars were—but definitely not his family. It was as if he begrudged us anything that might have made our lives easier or a bit enjoyable. It was all so confusing for children who had no one to turn to—no one to confide in. It was tragic. I find it impossible to fully and accurately describe the situation because so much of the harm done lay in the feelings that he evoked. These feelings I hid deep within my psyche—festering memories that have haunted me throughout my life.

On days when we could sleep in, and Dad was at home, he had this spiteful habit of getting up early and clanging the pots and pans on the stove to wake us all. Then he'd go back to bed: his job was done. He had disturbed the whole house.

My father had no respect for women. Did he hate them? Perhaps. This was evident in the way he treated his wife. She was there to serve him. Not to be loved and cherished. Not to be looked after. He had no qualms about sitting back and letting her fetch wood and water. He seldom offered to do such jobs even when the kids were not around to do these chores. Children too were of little value. They were "a dime a dozen" as the saying goes. But as we grew older we had some worth; we became useful. We could carry the wood and water. And soon, we could feed the pigs and go to the pasture to bring the cows home and milk them. We could give them hay and clean their stalls. But above all, we could feed his hunting hounds. They deserved extra care.

Even in later years, after most of the older sibling had left home, my father's hounds remained a daily source of contention. "Some things never change." The severity of his repeated tirades—his verbal and mental abuse—cannot be glossed over and must not be minimized. Any attempt by me to convey in words the depth of the destruction he wrought would fall far short of reality. He would still come home from work and begin his usual relentless tirade. "Have you fed the dogs? If you don't feed those dogs, you might as well go out and shoot them." Words cannot describe the damage done by this "crazy-making" because it lies deep in the psyche—in the feelings that will be passed on to the next generation—if no one is strong enough and determined enough to break the cycle. One day, my brother took the gun and went out and shot the dogs. Everyone has a breaking point. But for a child to be driven to that place by his father is contemptible. It's criminal.

I never had a real relationship with my father. Not then. Not ever. To me he was, what I gradually became in childhood, a non-person. Years later, in therapy, I always had trouble describing him. In my mind, he defied description. It was as if, to me, he had never really existed as a person. Or perhaps I feared that, in describing him, the hate would show through. It seemed, for the most part, that I blotted him out of my memory, yet the feelings remained smoldering destructively within me. As important as they were to my recovery, I did not talk about them; I did not disclose such things. My pain was excruciating, but my shame was greater. Family secrets must be kept secret. The toxic shame that lived in me, that shaped my being, must not be put into words. It must be lived—in secret.

This was so much a part of what rendered me mentally ill—what "drove me crazy." And even still, as I write this, I feel somewhat like a traitor. Those feelings which once lay beyond words can still cause my heart to cringe and bring tears to my eyes. Some things one does not forget—if not the fact, the feeling.

Today, even from my perspective as an adult, I would describe my father in one word—*evil*. And if he wasn't evil, his actions definitely were—a subtle difference I find hard to discern. This is my perception, not a judgement. It is not for me to judge.

Do I have any happy memories of my father—few, if any, that I remember.

The last time I saw my father he was in the hospital. The cancer had spread and he could not speak, and I had nothing to say. I stood by his bedside, immobilized. I did not cry; I had long since shed all my tears for him during all my growing-up years. I could not bring myself to touch him. I did not kiss him goodbye; we had never really said, "Hello."

Since then I have changed. I have learned to forgive. I have regrets.

Siblings

Am I "my brother's keeper?" Different family members, although living in the same household, experience events differently as they happen within the family. We are each uniquely predisposed to the impacts of childhood and life in general. If each of the ten siblings in my family were asked to describe their childhood, each one of us would have a different story, a different point of view, a different reality, even to the extent that it would sound as if we each had been raised in a different home. Family secrets resonate differently with different people, and these happenings from the past define our present and our future.

I write from my perspective, from my personal reality. I write from the depths of my being where, as a sensitive child, I was so adversely impacted that I would fight depression for the rest of my life. That is how my well of childhood feelings was filled—with murky, toxic memories—a damning testament to my upbringing.

Some say we live our heaven or hell here on earth—that's questionable. But if my childhood wasn't hell, in my mind at least, it was purgatory.

To dispel the painful reality of our childhood, some members of the family would say, "That's not true; that's not the way it was; that didn't happen; everybody lived like that." They create their reality to help them cope, to accept what was unacceptable.

On the other hand, another member of the family has said, "Diane, you don't know the half of it. It was much worse. My story would be far more revealing, if I ever decided to write it." Among my worries during those childhood days was my fear for my siblings. One particular sibling was defiant, grounded and self-assured. I was submissive. How could one person in this family grow up mentally healthy when no one had any idea how sick I was.

I always thought that my brothers had it easier than the girls. They could get out of the house more; remove themselves from the chaos within it. I was wrong. They were part of it. They, too, were victims of violence. They, too, grew up with the scars of battle that our childhood inflicted upon us. They, too, have their demons to fight.

They say that telling your life story over and over is therapeutic. But we never experienced that healing power of storytelling in our family. We never talked much in such a manner, or to any extent, that I remember. We were each entombed in our own cocoon, for the most part, out of reach of others and trusting no one. Our stories lay buried deep within us, unspoken. It was as if we didn't have any connection or real interest in each other. We were not our "brother's keeper." We were each carrying more pain than we could handle.

This all happened so long ago, so why, oh why, are these tears in my eyes?

CHAPTER 6

Farmhouse No. 1

Part 1

My three older siblings were born in a hospital because, during that time, my family was living in a town which had such a facility. But before I was born, my father moved the family into the bush, to isolation. He didn't consider how his young family would cope and the hardships this move would impose upon anyone, including his wife.

A woman is subject to her husband—so the Bible says. My mother was a submissive woman with the old-fashioned ideology that a wife follows where her husband leads. She suffered her whole life because of this belief.

The "new" home was three miles from a town with a church that we faithfully attended each Sunday. The town also had a grocery store but no hospital. In the next town over, which was ten miles away, there was a private home where expectant mothers went toward the end of their pregnancy. There was no hospital in this town, only a doctor who worked in an "outpost." Deliveries took place there. This is where I and my three younger siblings were born.

I started my education in a little one room country school house. Kindergarten was yet unheard of. We had one teacher for grades one through eight, which was not out of the ordinary in those days. I found myself, like most of the students, part of an "in-between generation"—the generation caught between our Polish ancestry and the English school system. My parents spoke both Polish and English, and my oldest brother and sister spoke some Polish early on but lost it as they got older. I understand very little Polish and I have never spoken it. The mixture of the two languages spoken at home and at school, created problems for me with phonics and pronunciation. I emerged from this dilemma with an odd "accent" that was hard to pinpoint—merely bad pronunciation, I was later told.

Attending school was a source of overwhelming anxiety for me. I felt it to the pit of my stomach. I did not fit in. The other students seemed strange to me, as if they belonged to another world. Or was I the one who belonged to another world? I protected myself with silence when I could not deal with the stark reality of everyday life and I tried to disappear from the frightful world around me.

Throughout grades one to five, I seldom spoke in class. I preferred not to talk to avoid possible embarrassment. I felt stupid, ignorant, unlikeable. I felt like a "nothingness." I lived in fear that someone might talk to me or ask me something and I wouldn't know what to say. I had nothing to say. My whole life was a "nothingness." I felt like I knew nothing—especially about the outside world. We never really talked at home. Mostly we just yelled at each other, or at least that's how my child's mind remembers it. I lived in constant fear of being "found out"—a traumatizing, shameful fear. Everyone at school knew I could talk. It just took me many years to feel comfortable or brave enough in the school setting to speak.

I was beyond being shy. I was passive, withdrawn, and robot like in my actions. I did exactly as I was told and never ventured "outside the lines." One extremely cold winter day, I got to school feeling frozen. The teacher told me to sit in a chair which she had put beside the wood stove. I sat there and I sat there. I remember, at one point, putting my hand up and touching my bobby pins and they burned my fingers. She hadn't told me to move, to take my own seat—so I didn't move. I was overly obedient—inhibited—there was no *"me."* I always wished I could hide, disappear, just become invisible. This was the beginning of the protective shell I would build around myself.

My family had very limited contact with the outside world. Although I did not understand why, they insinuated that other people—all those people "out there"—were the "enemy." That's the way my family treated other people and that was the feeling in our house. I lived with fear of that mysterious outside world. Even my fellow pupils were part of the "enemy." Where were my friends? I had none. So much I cried.

During these first five years, I walked to school with my two older brothers and a sister. My mother had become fearful of being alone at home with the younger kids and often kept one of us older ones at home. My sister, who is three years younger than me, was kept home until she was eight. She was company for Mom and helped look after the babies. To this day she claims that, until we moved to our next house—almost as far in the bush as the first one—no one in the outside world knew that she existed. When school and church authorities discovered her, they confronted our parents, and she finally started school in the spring of the year she turned eight. Thankfully, she had wanted to go to school so badly, she had learned enough from those of us who were in school that the principal put her ahead into grade two. In reality, however under normal circumstances, she would have gone into grade three.

But there was little that was normal in our lives or in our way of living. This delay in starting her education had long-lasting effects on my sister and her future family. And it was an unbelievably cruel and selfish act on the part of our mother.

As a child, I totally lacked my sister's resiliency, and I shudder to think of what would have happened to me if I had been the child that had been kept home for years. How much did anyone know about this world we lived in, about the world that I lived in?

Part 2

I remember the farmhouse we lived in during this time, from my birth until I was almost eleven. The house was square with a four-sided roof. It was a gloomy blackish grey with the unpainted look of barn wood. On one side a "summer kitchen" with a rough unfinished floor which was always dirty, had been added. On that same side of the house but a short distance away, was a string of equally bleak buildings: the milk house, the barn, the woodshed, and the outhouse.

In the summer, this additional kitchen was cooler and breezier than the house itself and gave us much needed space. Our windows had no screens, so, there were always flies everywhere. We'd hang up fly stickers and "smudges" and use fly swatters all the time, but the flies always won the battle. In the winter, they died away or hibernated, but the price we paid was enormous.

The winters were bitterly cold and seemed endless. During these months, the metal pail with our drinking water and the basin of water in which we washed would both be covered with a layer of ice each morning. Our two wood-burning stoves were our only source of heat. One stove was for heat alone while the other was also for cooking and had a tank for heating water. There were also heavy irons that were heated and used to iron the few Sunday clothes that we had. After all, we had to look respectable for church. When it came to washing clothes, much more water had to be heated atop the stove. Mom's motor-run wash machine broke down regularly so the scrubbing board got a lot of use.

When we went to bed at night we could see our breath so we'd pull the blankets over our heads to feel its warmth. The house was not insulated, and the cracks in the walls were filled with everything from rags, to clay, and even cow dung. Still, the wind whistled and the snow swirled through the cracks and into the house and sprayed around us as we slept.

In these winters during my early years my two sisters and I slept together, with our snowsuits on, in hopes of keeping warm. But it was impossible to feel warm ever. The coldness seemed to emanate from within me.

Chimney fires were not out of the ordinary. Apparently, the solution was to pour some water into the stove causing steam to rise which would put the fire out. How we survived any of this is beyond my comprehension.

But we didn't know anything different. Didn't everyone live like this? How were we to know? Locked in our life of seclusion, other people, their homes and their way of living, were unknown to us. They were the "others" out there—"the enemy". It was years before I was socialized enough and brave enough to have anything to do with the "others". It spanned my entire childhood and stretched into my adult life.

These were the years towards the end of the Great Depression. No one was immune to its scarcity. Our food was simple and basic. We grew staples like potatoes and vegetables and we baked bread almost daily. Things like cabbage were always plentiful, so Mom made sauerkraut in barrels. Pork and fish were salted and also stored in ceramic barrels. In the fall, my father and his hunting and drinking buddies usually shot a deer or two—some of which my mother canned. To this day, I can't stand the taste of venison.

I remember pork or fish and potatoes and gravy and vegetables. Sometimes, the vegetables were even creamed. Those were the good old days, when there was food on the table. But there were times when bread and lard with a bit of sugar—or even a sprinkle of salt for a change—helped keep us fed. Blackstrap molasses was a treat. It must have been cheap.

In the summer, food was somewhat more plentiful. There were apples and rhubarb and we picked berries as best as young kids can. I cringe when I think of the blueberry patches around the rock piles. Before picking, we'd throw stones against the rocks to chase the snakes away. That did little to alleviate my fear. Still, I had to pick berries. Soon the job of picking berries became an escape—part of "my other world".

We all had very little. A meager existence. While love is boundless and makes hard times bearable, what set my family apart was the lack of love, and the emptiness that created. I developed an over-whelming sense of loneliness and hopelessness which turned into, the simmering hate of anger.

Part 3

A small stream wound its way around two sides of the house and disappeared somewhere beyond where my feet had ventured. There was a makeshift bridge we crossed to get to the school which we could see in the distance. Other than the schoolhouse, there were no signs of civilization within our view from home. We had our immediate space for house and garden, which we also used for play. Further out there were hayfields and pastures. Beyond that, trees edged our view enshrouding us with their perimeter. On the other side of the house was a sturdier bridge that we had to cross to get to town, the grocery store, and church.

During summer holidays, some of us kids walked to the church to attend catechism classes. It was three miles away. It was my brother's job to get me safely to the church and back. I was young, depressed, and not very observant. As many days as we made the trip, I never learned the way. To add to my confusion, my brother would take shortcuts across farmers' fields and through the bush which added to my fear of the unknown. That was pretty much the extent of the world I lived in for the first eleven years of my life. I had withdrawn into a world of my own making to help cope with my anxieties and to create a sense of security as best I could. It was my way of dealing with the raw feelings of childhood.

We were left to make our own fun. Unfortunately, it felt, more often than not, that it was not only us against the outside world, but us against each other. There was an underlying anger and hos-tility that had been nurtured into us. It ruled our world. And yet we played. We fished in the stream, within view of the house, and picked cranberries along its marshy shore even though we were warned that there was quicksand. We would get very wet, but we never found any quicksand. Blurred in my mind is a game called "Auntie Over." It consisted of throwing a ball over the house or over the shed which was much lower and easier, and as we threw, we'd call "Auntie, Auntie-I-Over" to warn the person on the other side. If the ball failed to clear the building and came back to us, we'd yell "Back in the Clover." I have no idea what the purpose or goal of this game was!

From somewhere, maybe from the stream by the house, Dad would get brown burlap, potato bags full of fish—suckers. He would gut and wash them by the side of the bridge, and we'd get to play with some parts of their insides that floated like balloons downstream. A crude sort of play, but at the time, it seemed fun nonetheless.

My older brothers had another field of play. They would take the .22 rifle and go hunting for partridge or rabbits, or anything they happened to see that moved, like squirrels and birds. My hunting was mostly for things like four-leaf clovers or flowers like wild daisies so I could remove the petals one by one, reciting "he loves me he loves me not." I have no idea how this started. I had no idea what love was!

I soaked up the warmth of the summer days, which seemed so sunny and long. I enjoyed the fields of wild flowers which gave such beauty to our otherwise drab surroundings. In flowerbeds beside the house, Mom would plant snapdragons and hollyhocks and, her always favourite, geraniums. I loved the outdoors. There were some happy times when I was able to come out of my shell and enjoy what would inevitably be passing seasonal distractions, moments when I could almost forget. Inside, however, I always knew these happy times would not last—they never did.

One of our chores, from spring into the fall, was to drag pails full of dirty diapers down to the stream. At the stream we would rinse out the diapers, rubbing them on the rocks to clean them as one would have done in a third-world country. Mother warned us not to let the diapers go and lose them—never did she caution us not to fall in. Years later, we questioned, "Was losing a diaper more terrible than the prospect of losing a child?" Perhaps it was best we had no such thoughts at the time.

When winter came we were confined indoors for the most part. There were two rooms downstairs and three makeshift bedrooms upstairs. It was chaos—much worse than summertime. Play was limited to indoors—there were no puzzles, no cards, no board games, no

TV nor any electronics. There was only homework done by dim coal oil lamps, there was the incessant bickering and fighting amongst the siblings, and the endless barking of orders from Mom and Dad to shut up, to do this, or to do that, with the often added incentive of a slap on the head. There was no peace, no quiet, no normal conversation, no feelings of love or unity; no meaningful anything—just more "nothingness."

Despite the cold, there were still chores to be done around the house and stables. Sometimes we would play in the barn. We would hide in the hay, or jump from the loft. The snow also had to be shoveled so that was sometimes a source of play as well. When the stream froze over, a space was shoveled off and we played shinny hockey. I had never seen a live hockey game, but we had skates of sorts and sticks. Why? Because Dad was a hockey fan. What he wanted, he got. And he wanted his sons to play hockey.

On paper it sounds like an ideal childhood except for the lonely, wounded child who lived within me. She knew the emotional pain of "lovelessness." She felt the fears and anxieties of an unprotected child in a world of utter confusion. She lived the hopelessness of poverty and isolation. She lived in helplessness in a world beyond her control. She was so young and she was so old. She learned to hate. She felt despair.

No "I AM-ness"

When we are robbed of ourselves,
we are robbed of everything.

—Goethe

Emotional and spiritual wounds ran deep in my family. I had no sense of "I AM-ness." I had no way of knowing who I was or what I should be. I tried hard never to draw attention to myself. I just wanted to hide from the world; not to be noticed. I just wanted to disappear into the woodwork; not to be seen. Even as I grew older I never developed a sense of *"me."* I was completely disconnected. In my mind there was no *"me"* and I wished to become invisible to hide my "nothingness." I identified so deeply with this desire that I became what I wished for. I achieved my childhood goal; I became an "invisible person." That became my identity, and for years to come, I lived up to that identity. In counseling, many years later I learned that the psychiatric term for this phenomenon really is "invisible person." In my layman's language I was a "non-person." There was no *"me."* I did not exist.

Not knowing who you are is among the greatest of life's tragedies.

I was never a child. I always felt the weight of adult responsibilities. I was young and yet so very mature but only in the way that I coped with those adult responsibilities thrust upon me. I felt I had to do as much as I possibly could to help around the house. No one had to tell me what to do and there was always work to be done. I was programmed from childhood to serve—to look after others. I could sacrifice myself without even knowing it or caring. I never had to be yelled at to do my chores, and I never talked back. I was too afraid. When I grew big enough I was recruited into carrying wood and water and milking cows, when needed. It was an automatic response—an adult response. The feeling of staying busy, insinuated itself in me. I began to feel that I must always be busy always doing something.

When siblings squabbled I would do whatever was necessary to appease others. I always took the path of least resistance. In my case—passivity was my response. On the outside I might have been considered the perfect child. In reality I became what I would call an adult/child.

I learned to control everything I could possibly control. I was a loner and very independent. I looked after myself: my hair, my clothes, my neatness, and I helped look after the younger kids. However, there was no one to look after me. When I had needs, there was no one there to fill them so I didn't ask. There was really no one to talk to—to confide in—no one to take my hand and guide me in any of my life passages. There were no hugs, no "good night" kisses, no shared whispered secrets. At bedtime, the coal oil lamp was blown out, and there was darkness in my room like the darkness in my heart. It felt good to cry myself to sleep; it eased the pain, if only slightly and only for a little while. I cried most every night, but no one ever listened. No one seemed to care.

As children, we did very little to console each other. We hadn't been taught about caring and compassion and we hadn't experienced it. We each lived in our own little cocoon of self defenses built up since birth to ward off the hurt of our hostile world. There was no support from our mother; she was lost in her own world of depression and survival. My defense became an impenetrable wall built by my fears and pain, my anger and hate, behind which I disappeared whenever I felt overwhelmed, which happened all too often. It was my blanket of steel in which I wrapped myself when life became more than I could bear in my "aloneness."

When a child is forced to learn, at an early age, to take care of themselves, they also fall into a pattern of thinking that they have to do it all by themselves. A child learns one of two basic attitudes: "I have needs and I have the power to get them met" or "I have needs and I am powerless to get them met." The necessary love, care, and validation was missing in my life as a child so I never learned to identify and express my needs. I never developed a sense of *"me."* I moved through childhood and well into adulthood feeling powerless, empty and apathetic. It was the "nothingness" known as chronic depression.

Unknown

I know what it's like to know yet not to know. I have a memory of the time when my mother lost a full-term baby boy. I don't remember the details of the event—that's all a blur. Things of this nature weren't talked about, but my young uneducated child mind sensed the tragedy. I was old enough for an explanation; old enough to be told what had happened. But, no one said a word.

We had one car which Dad drove to work each day, and in those days, we still had no phone. When Mom began to hemorrhage, my brother ran the three miles into town for help. It was too late to save the baby. I knew, but I was not told.

While Mom was away in the hospital, I cleaned the house as usual—an obsessive compulsive habit that had developed from a very early age. I found my mother's bloodied skirt buried in the bottom of the laundry basket where she had tried to hide it. I remember that someone made a tiny wooden box as a coffin for the baby, and I remember that Dad took the day off work, dressed up in his suit, and went into town.

What I understood clearly was that he—my brother—wasn't baptized, so according to the church laws at the time, he could not be buried in the church's graveyard, instead he was buried outside of the graveyard. He did not belong. I could identify with that. I felt like I did not belong anywhere.

Religion can be so cruel, and life can be even crueler when no one talks, when no one explains and when no one shows they care.

When I was in my sixties the daughter of a friend of mine gave birth to a stillborn child. They acknowledged that it was a tragic event. They mourned the loss of a child—a human being. They weren't afraid to talk and to cry. And I cried with them. Some of the tears were belated for the brother I had never met—never seen—whose name I had never heard and for whom I had never properly grieved. I cried at these thoughts but was comforted by the words of the Prophet Jeremiah.

"Before I formed you in the womb I knew you."

Omissions

If there is such a thing as lying or sinning by omission—and I firmly believe there is—it would cover all that I should have been told as I entered my teenage years.

I experienced the humiliation of getting my first period at school as a twelve-year-old grade seven student with no resources and too steeped in shame to seek help from anyone. Menstruation was one of the things not spoken of at home. Sex and sexuality were shrouded in secrecy and myths and shame. Thankfully, I had learned about menstruation from my older sister. I even remember the little booklet that she gave me, *Growing Up and Liking It.* I didn't like it at all! I didn't even like the thought. But I have never forgotten that title!

At that time, when I read the book, I begged God to please let me not start my period until I was at least sixteen or more. I didn't think I could cope with one more thing. So when it happened, I cried incessantly and refused to tell anyone why; even my sister could not console me. I felt that God had let me down. I felt that he was punishing me for something I had done—for all the bad, shameful, impure, unforgivable sins I had committed. I was guilty. I was despicable. I felt so sinful and so alone. This was the vengeful God I had learned about in church and at catechism class. There was no one I trusted enough to turn to in Heaven or on earth. It is very difficult to trust anyone when you grow up trusting no one.

Ours was a shame-based world. In our world of sarcasm, crude jokes, and foul language, bodily functions were seen as shameful—dirty and degrading. Under normal circumstances, I was an easy target for embarrassment, my brothers saw to that. How could I cope with hiding one more secret?

> I came upon you when you were magical
> Before you could know I was there
> I severed your soul
> I pierced you to the core
> I brought you feelings of being
> flawed and defective
> I brought you feelings of distrust,
> ugliness, stupidity, doubt
> Worthlessness, inferiority, and unworthiness
> I made you feel different
> I told you there was something wrong with you
> I soiled your Godlikeness My
> name is Toxic Shame
> —Leo Booth but reworked in
> "Homecoming" by John Bradshaw

I remember so well milking my cow and leaning my head against her as I sobbed. She seemed to feel and understand my pain, my tears, and sense my need and she stood especially quiet as I cried.

I was at the mercy of my emotions—a vulnerable child, now turned woman, on the edge of despair. Years later I was not surprised to learn that a lack of appropriate instruction about sex is, in itself, a form of abuse. How could it be otherwise?

Adolescence

Adolescence can be a difficult time for many young people. It can bring with it distressing feelings of loneliness and isolation because they often think they are the only ones who suffer. It's not just a "poor people" problem though. Even those from well-to-do, educated families experience painful memories. Money, love, and education do not shield people from the pains of growing up. I had neither money, nor love, nor the education factor. My childhood pangs were magnified. I had the added burden of childhood abuses, depression, and feelings of toxic shame. These were the taunting companions that accompanied me throughout childhood and for many years that followed.

As I grew up, I always intuitively sensed that there was something wrong with me, my family, and the way we lived. I was right in so many ways I just didn't know exactly what it was. Poverty and squalor already defined us, which caused long lasting effects on all of the children. No one spoke about it or admitted it or pointed out the ways in which we were different. I always felt there was something missing; something lacking in some way.

The older I got the more these feelings intensified. As unobservant as I was, I did notice that there were people who were carefree and happy. But then, I knew nothing about their private lives, their hidden anxieties and problems—what they had to contend with each day. I just wanted to be like them. But for me, life was such a struggle both at home and at school. I lived burdened with feelings of distrust, worthlessness, and a keen sense of the ugliness of our lives. And springing from my insecurities was a desperate need for order in my life—a sort of armor to protect myself from the judgements of others.

At a very young age I developed an obsessive compulsive disorder—I became a perfectionist and a clean freak. Consequently, everything became a problem, from what clothes to wear, how to comb my hair, what to say, how to sit, or how much time to spend on my homework. I was meticulous and I did everything to the best of my ability. This perfectionism has stayed with me for most of my life. The desire to control things drove me to do endless household chores, or ensure that I helped out as best I could. There were always dishes to be washed, floors to be swept, meals to be made, and clothes to be washed and hung out or brought in. There was water and wood to be carried, cows to be milked, and feed and stalls to be cleaned out. During my years at home there was always a baby in the house that needed to be cared for. This meant endless dirty bottles and diapers.

At times, I was overwhelmed by the grossness of our life. One particularly salient memory was the baby's bed. The inadequate circumstances that we had to cope with included feces laden dirty diapers, urine soaked pads and blankets and mattresses, that resulted in maggots in the bedding. In the winter, the mattress and all would be put outside in the cold to kill the larvae. In the summer, the same mattress and bedding would be put in the sun to dry and get rid of the maggots. So much I remember. So much I've tried to forget. I still cringe.

At a very young age, I took on the task of ironing clothes. Maybe no one cared, but my clothes had to be neat. With no sense of internal self this was essential to my outward facade. I also felt that the way other members of my family looked reflected on me. So young, to be so concerned with outward appearances. In time, I ironed anything that I thought needed ironing. I became good at it. It helped me feel productive in my world of lonely "lovelessness." It was therapeutic and more rewarding than sweeping floors and washing dishes. From my limited contact with other people, this seemed normal, but it wasn't long before it became a habit.

During my teenage years, there were a couple of boys who showed an interest in me. I looked upon them with disdain and treated them accordingly. What could they possibly see in me? How could they be so stupid as to even notice me, let alone like me? There was nothing about me that was attractive, worthy of anyone's attention, affection or time.

I wasn't pretty like the other girls and I didn't have nice clothes. I wasn't cute and giggly and talkative. Having had so little contact with the real world, I had nothing to talk about. What happened in my family, on the farm, was securely locked within me. It was sealed in secrecy and shame.

In a way, I was mature beyond my years and yet I was naïve and knew little about the real world, people, and socializing. I found it hard to relate to other people, even those my own age. I had never so much as carried on a conversation with an adult! I had a skewed perception of life. I maintained a stoic face for the outside world but inside I was trembling tearful child.

CHAPTER 11

Farmhouse No. 2

Part 1

We moved to a bigger farmhouse the year that I started grade six. We were still more than three miles from the nearest town and almost as isolated as we had been in our previous home. Luckily the town had a hospital, where the last three of my siblings were born, and there was a school that provided grades one to ten. As I recall it had at least four classrooms and four teachers, even a principal and an office, which doubled as the library, with a limited number of books. There were two grocery stores in town which really didn't matter because we still lived in poverty and deprivation.

Our so-called farm, like the last one, was a farm in name only, but we were now lumped in with "the farm kids" who were bussed to school. This, in itself, felt degrading. It wasn't really a school bus, but rather, a converted van with doors at the back and wooden benches inside along each side. I don't remember windows; it's possible there were none. We were a somber bunch as we sat facing each other with pained expressions and troubled thoughts. Most of us were Polish. Maybe that didn't matter much to others, but already in my mind, it was a stigma, and that was a feeling that stayed with me throughout my young life. I was in my teens before I realized that the strangers in town who were referred to as "DPs from the old country" were really "Displaced Persons" and not "Dumb Polacks." I knew nothing about other people and places.

Our new home required us to walk three-quarters of a mile to catch the school bus. The gravel road went up and down hills and through the bush to where it met the main county road. Rarely did a day go by that I wasn't crying by the time I left home. But I knew exactly at what bend in the road, at what hill, I had to force my tears to stop so that I could pull myself together and put on my outward "mask" before reaching the bus and being seen by the other kids. I hid my pain to the outside world and I learned to live with that lump in my throat—that lump that forms when you're trying really hard not to cry.

For years, the only reading materials that came into the house were our school books and Dad's newspaper. And sometimes, even he knew nothing about anyone or anything mentioned in it. As I got older, I read library books from school, as time permitted, and anything else I could get my hands on. Somehow, somewhere, I discovered the *Reader's Digest*. I devoured the stories and devoutly took on challenges such as "increase your word power." I developed a vocabulary beyond my age and grade and while I understood the words and knew their meaning—I had never heard many of them spoken aloud. And so pronunciation was a problem when I went to use them. The "th" sound was the worst for me. "Think" would come out as "tink" and "tank" for "thank" and so on. I spoke English as if it were my second language. Often, I was made fun of because of my odd pronunciation. Surely, through the years, I must have been taught phonics. Yet I really never learned how to sound out words properly. In spelling class, I didn't sound out words, I memorized them.

Still I was an excellent student. I had to excel to prove myself. However, I was extremely sensitive, obedient, and intense. I loved books and learning. My school work was my escape. I found a place to hide in my studies, but I also found amazing and sustaining grace, as well as support for my survival. Words helped to take my mind and attention off myself and my home life. In my books I could escape from the real world and live in a different one—one more to my own liking. I put a lot of pressure on myself as I strove for perfection, and sometimes even perfection wouldn't do, but books gave me a reprieve, at least for a little while.

I had always been extremely self-conscious and talked very little. But by the time I reached grade six, I could no longer avoid talking in class. I became a little more social, although I always felt I had nothing to say. I lacked all sense of self and so my self-image was dependent on my outward appearance—the façade I presented to the outside world. I became a great actress. Unfortunately, I had developed a deep-rooted inferiority complex. I was plagued by feelings of being different, somehow lacking what other pupils had. How could I become like them, not even as they really were, but as I perceived them to be—happy, perfect? I always felt that others were more deserving and so much better than I was and I lived that way. Was there a secret? If so, what was it? Who could tell me? Where could I find it? I searched for years to come, without success.

Still, I cried, I cried so much. Often, my cries reverberated deep inside of me where I stifled the feelings and internalized the pain. Throughout my life these suppressed feelings erupted like mini volcanoes of anger, but no one understood—not even me—as I lived behind my endless masks. To my shame and humiliation, my brothers acted out their anger and pain. They externalized their feelings. This was intensified by the lack of discipline and the fact that there were, in our house, none of the normal distractions to break the bleak reality of life. There was no electricity, no TV, no money, no love, no nothing; only my brothers' anger and cursing and fighting. Where does a child go when there's no place to go? I escaped within. I internalized the complete chaos and hopelessness of a life beyond my control. I was so ashamed of my brothers. I had now reached an age where I wished I wasn't related to any of them. This wish, I placed with my other wish—the wish that I were dead. I may have even wished that they were dead.

These damning wishes were so much a part of my childhood—secrets I kept locked within my heart. These feelings worsened when

I entered my teenage years. I don't know how many times I'd tell myself, "when I get out of here, life will be different." I wasn't sure how it would happen. I didn't realize that I carried all those feelings of my abused and wounded child within me because that is where she and my memories were formed, that pile of unforgettable memories. I didn't know that wherever I went, they would be with me.

It is only after years of counseling and soul searching and plain old hard work that I can see clearly enough to put any of this into words. It has taken me all of these years to get past the pain and to understand and validate the feelings. It has taken all of these years to breathe.

Part 2

The second farmhouse felt less isolated than the first one because it was situated on a hill. We could see our neighbours a mile across the way, even if we rarely visited them. Their house was a sign of life out there. I loved our location because I could watch the sunrise above the hill at the back of the house, even from my bedroom window; and then, at day's end, I could climb that hill to watch the sunsets across what I called "the valley." Up on the hill, there was a huge rock which was my vantage point. From there, I watched countless sunsets—always in my "aloneness."

On this farm there was more open space and more opportunities for distractions—anything that broke the boredom of our lives was welcomed. Distractions were our play and recreation. In the spring, we'd splash, barefoot, through the water that ran down the hill behind the house. It became a tradition of sorts, our yearly ritual. In front of the house were two cedar trees. Somewhere we managed to find a hammock and string it up between the trees. Then we fought to see who could lie in it. There were times when I was alone and I'd lie there peacefully and undisturbed. On Easter morning, we'd get up early so as not to miss the sunrise. We were told that, on Easter morning, the sun would dance. I can't say it ever happened, perhaps in my imagination.

My favourite part about this house was the verandah. It ran around two sides of the house, had a railing around it and a roof. It was not used as a patio would be used today. We had no family gatherings, no barbecues. Mostly we just played out there. We could run the length of the verandah, jump over the railing at the other end, and head for the barn. Or, sometimes we would run past the Delco shed and the wood shed and head toward the bush up the hill. Closer to the house we played Cowboys and Indians. While this would no longer be considered politically correct, back then it was a favourite game of ours. We would stealthily sneak through the trees and crawl through the underbrush. All this would be done with a posse or the Lone Ranger in hot pursuit.

My bedroom window opened onto the roof of a porch. During the summer, I'd crawl out onto the roof and just lie in the sun—enjoy the view—or read. I could also get down from the roof to the ground, but I couldn't crawl back up. This was probably as adventurous as I was capable of as a child. It helped pass time and got me out of the house, which was a blessing.

One of my greatest delights was sitting on the verandah with a book or gazing out to watch the sunset. It touched my soul and transported me to places beyond the house.

Often, as dusk turned to evening, I'd lean on the railing, watching for the first star to make its appearance so I could pray my simple rhyme. "Star light, star bright, first star I see tonight, I wish you may, I wish you might, grant this wish I wish tonight." So many silent stars passed by; so many childish wishes not granted. Years of wishes, all washed away by tears.

Gradually, countless stars would stud the darkening sky. It was time to leave my observatory. This outside life was my reprieve. I'd go inside to face my next chore—making lunches for the gang. Why was it my job? I'm not sure. Probably because I was the responsible one and didn't have to be reminded and harped at to get it done. But it can be very hard to make lunches out of nothing, which was sometimes the case. Bread and jam was the usual. It wasn't real jam, it was mostly pectin, but it was sweet, and, it was better than nothing. Sometimes, we had bologna or peanut butter. Then there were times when there was no wax paper to wrap the sandwiches in, and I'd be lucky to find a paper bag to put them in. It all reinforced in me the relentless feelings of poverty. It didn't matter to my brothers. They'd often just go down to the grocery store at the bottom of the hill and steal bananas or other items. Each of us did what we needed to do, in our own way, to survive.

My next job came with morning. Since I was the first one awake and downstairs I would wake the other kids before heading to the barn to milk my cow. My sisters weren't so bad, but with my brothers, I had to be persistent. Often, I'd end up hitting the ceiling with the broom handle as a last resort to get them out of bed. Often they'd come down in a foul mood and miss the bus anyway. It didn't occur to me to just let them sleep in and suffer the consequences. This job itself was depressing. No one else seemed to care if they got to school, so why did I? Was I the only responsible one? Or would I have felt humiliated? By this age, I was ashamed of my brothers in many ways, and it only got worse as I grew older.

It's possible that we were as happy as kids like us, in our circumstance, were capable of being. But under the circumstances, it was hard for any feelings of happiness to make a lasting impression. There were times when I laughed and played; when I at least, appeared normal. But I always knew it would not last. It never did. I had learned that from sad experience. "Be wary of feeling too happy because those feelings of depression and hopelessness always come back." They always did. And then it would feel much worse, much more oppressive. Underneath my many masks, depression progressed in its stealthy, silent manner. Even when it overflowed, nobody seemed to notice, confirming my "nothingness."

Part 3

At this second farmhouse we called the shed that housed the power generator the "Delco" shed. When the Delco, a power generator, was working, we had electricity, or at least lights for which the farmhouse was wired, and cold water piped into a single, deep, utility sink. Oddly enough, the sink wasn't in the kitchen. Instead, it was situated at the bottom of the stairs in the hallway which led to the back door. But as time passed and the Delco broke down more and more often, our father, an excellent mechanic, just stopped fixing it. Then we were back to coal oil lamps and lanterns and carrying water. We didn't deserve electricity, and so we lived without it. It was all just a part of the darkness in our lives. We were all adversely impacted, especially our mother. Unfortunately she never stood up for herself or for her kids, then again if she had, she might have been slapped.

This house, like the last one, had little insulation. Like before, our only source of heat was our kitchen stove and a heater stove in the living room. We also had what we called a "summer kitchen," which was actually another room at the side of the house. It, too, had a cooking stove, but this room could only be used in the summertime. Whether or not it was cooler, I'm not sure. Most of the floor was softwood, which seemed to attract dirt and would soak up the water when we washed it, or should I say when I washed it? The quarter of the floor that was hardwood was much easier to wash, even though floors didn't stay clean for long with so many kids running in and out. During the winter, this kitchen became a junk room which, as usual, I tried to keep clean in spite of the cold.

With no real insulation, the winters were bitterly cold. We would lay rags or whatever was available across the bottom of the outside doors to keep the cold out. This helped somewhat, but on really cold nights, frost would cover these protective barriers. The doors didn't always stay closed properly, and locks were not a "thing", so we'd wedge knives between the door frames and the doors to keep the wind from blowing them open, especially during the night.

During the winter, Mom and the younger kids slept downstairs in part of the living room. I would have died before I gave up my privacy so I opted to stay upstairs.

Dad had the only bedroom that was heated. It was a small room, and the stovepipe from the heater stove ran through it. That stove was kept burning all night. My sister and I had the big bedroom which was always cold, although the pipe from the kitchen stove passed through it. The room was too big for the stovepipe alone to heat it. It also had three windows which added to the cold. Often, the kitchen stove would go out during the night leaving us without any heat whatsoever. In the bedroom, we could easily see our breath throughout most of the winter and our teeth would chatter and we'd shiver to our bones when changing our clothes. I would sometimes hold my clothes against the stovepipe to take the chill off before putting them on. At night time we would pile on more and more blankets and cover our heads, but the cold would come up even through the mattress. By morning, the weight of the blankets made our bodies ache. When Dad was away because of the weather, the older boys took over his bedroom. I never ever wanted it. I didn't want anything to do with him.

During the winter some of the windows frosted over completely. It was not just "the frost moved up the window pane, against the sun's advance." It was frost that could be there for months, and obstruct any view of the outside world. As kids do, we would scratch holes in it—possibly just from boredom—because there rarely was anything different to see outside. Throughout the winter, our slop water was carried out the door, across the width of the verandah, and thrown out near the steps. Depending on who was throwing it, it sometimes ended up near the steps. Over time it would build up into a hill of ugly, yellowish, frozen sludge. Sometimes, even the steps were covered with this yellow ice but then it had to be chipped off so we could get down the steps without slipping away.

In the winter, the road wasn't always plowed all the way to our house. This made the walk to the school bus a challenge. There were weeks when Dad couldn't drive home from the main road. He would come home carrying his case of beer and we children would walk back three-quarters of a mile to the car with a toboggan to bring back the groceries he had bought. "Only what is needed," he would always say. His beer could not be left to freeze. Our groceries didn't matter.

Three rows of hydro towers which we always referred to as "the hydro lines," ran close to our house, so close, and yet we had no electricity! They were the huge power lines that transport power from station to station, not house to house. They made a constant buzzing hum and I wouldn't dare touch them. My brothers, on the other hand, would attempt to climb them each summer.

In the winter, if the snow was not too deep, we'd walk along the hydro lines to a pond which we'd shovel off and play our version of hockey on. My brothers were lucky. They had a sport to play to break up the boredom of winter. They had hockey equipment and Dad, or their coach, even drove them to games. The girls had nothing of the sort. When we played our pond hockey games, we rounded up whatever winter clothes were available to keep warm, but it was always cold. At night we would play by the light of a lantern, and sometimes, even the moon. I didn't go very often. I hated the cold. It reminded me of my bedroom in the midst of winter. I didn't need reminders.

It was the same with sledding. I'd venture out but not for long and only if it were a beautiful starry night. I hated getting wet. To dry our clothes in the house, we'd hang them on ropes strung around the rooms. If the clothes were really wet and needed to be dry for school in the morning, we'd spread them on the heater stove. It had a black inner steel structure with a brown outer grill around it and on top of it. Of course, we had to stand and watch the clothes so that they wouldn't burn.

Playing in the snow banks or snowball fights was more of the same. While I liked the feel of sinking into the snow and crawling over the banks, or building igloos, once the cold and wet set in, the fun was gone. Then the job of drying clothes began. It just seemed like too much work. For me, it just wasn't worth it.

As much as I hated the cold of winter, I reveled in its innate beauty. Alone, I'd brave the cold of night to see the majestic sight of the moon sparkling diamonds on white fleece, or to see it stretch out a silver walkway on new fallen snow in front of me. I'd see the darkness of evergreen trees silhouetted against the moonlit sky. They seemed to move as the moon moved. I could find the North Star and the Big Dipper but other constellations had not yet been pointed out to me. Perhaps no one had cared enough to take the time to do so. By myself, I could never find them.

I'd gaze at stars, stars that seemed so near I felt that maybe— just maybe—I could reach up and touch them. But then, oh then, I might just taint their splendor. Those stars that seemed so close, I'd stand in awe and watch them sparkle like so many jewels suspended from the canopy of heaven.

But there were always the dark nights when nothing shone, not even in my soul. Where was God, or why was God in all of this?

Part 4

Our closest neighbour had children. One of them was a girl about my age. Occasionally, we'd play together. For years, this was the only person that I visited or who visited me. It was a blessing of sorts, even if we were shy and timid even with each other. I had a "friend," although I wasn't entirely sure that I knew what a friend was. It was years before I realized that my fellow pupils could be considered "friends." At the end of each school year in June, they'd stay in town, and I'd be back on the farm. So I questioned, "Are they friends?" How often do I have to see them? And how well do I have to know them? As I finished high school, I could count on my fingers the number of other people's houses that I had been in. And none of my friends, except the girl from across the way, had ever visited mine. Those years were so lonely.

I was in grade eight or nine before we finally got a telephone. Over the next few years, there were probably only three or four girls that I phoned. I had little to say. We had no TV, and I had no outside life except mass on Sundays, where there was little time to talk. School and homework were all we shared. Toward the end of one of my school years, the principal asked how my mother was doing and said she would visit us during the summer holidays. That would be a pleasant break in the monotony of our lives—a visitor. All summer I tried to keep the house clean—an almost impossible feat. I wanted it to be neat and tidy for when the principal came to visit. I waited all summer; she never came. The child in me died a little more.

Very few visitors ever came to our house. And I'd cringe with embarrassment when, occasionally, Dad would take someone on a grand tour of his great big house with its unmade beds, ratty, thread barren, barely usable sheets that were usually dirty, and secondhand blankets given to us by an uncle who worked in a textile mill, and clothes and junk everywhere. That was the upstairs. The kitchen and living room would be just as bad unless my sister and I had just been on one of our cleaning sprees. In that case, maybe, just maybe, the rooms might have been presentable. I was very conscious of cleanliness and tidiness, not only of my own person, but also of our house. Part of it was my perfectionist personality and part was my "perception" of what a house or home should look like. It definitely was not our reality. And the standard I sought was impossible. The only space I could control was my bedroom. If only I could have settled for that, life would have been much easier.

Am I Melodramatic?

There wasn't much out of the ordinary going on in our house on the winter day when I first threatened to commit suicide. I was about twelve years old. My mother had little control when fights broke out among my brothers. In critical moments, her yelling and screaming, her usual slaps, and even the razor strap, were ineffective. No real discipline had ever been established; neither had feelings of unity and love or mutual respect and familial bonds. No one in our family was their brother's keeper.

The confrontation had escalated from angry sarcasm, to cursing and swearing, to actual physical fighting. My brothers lashed out and cursed at each other because they felt that the world—life—lashed out at them, at us. For me, it was the feelings of anger and hopelessness with each of us against the other. This scene had played out many times during my young life. I cannot begin to describe the turmoil that raged within me or how their fighting impacted me. That particular day something within me just snapped. I didn't want to die. I just wanted the violence and the chaos, to stop. I just wanted to escape; to get away from the trauma of our lives. As I went out the door, in tears, into the bitter cold of midwinter, I announced that I was going to jump in the well. No one paid me heed.

Our well was open with a square wooden framework around the top, which we'd lean over when fetching water. It had a hinged wooden cover but didn't have a pump handle. Instead, it just had a long pole with a hook on the end of it on which we placed the pail to lower it down into the water, fill the pail, and pull it up. By this time in winter, the ice had built up in the well and the hole through which we lowered the pail to fill it had narrowed so that the pail barely passed through it.

Did I realize that if I jumped through that opening, I would not survive? God alone knows. Even though I didn't feel his presence that day, God most certainly was there, because I am here.

Perhaps it was fear, or my desire to live was greater than my need to escape the insanity in which we lived.

After sometime had passed, I'm told my mother sent one of my siblings out to check on me. I was lying in a snowbank sobbing as only an abandoned child in despair can sob. My pain overflowed. My tears did not stop then, not yet. They would not stop for years to come. By the time I left home I had shed more than a lifetime of tears. This was so long ago, and yet tears fill my eyes once again and my hands tremble.

It seems that almost everyone looks back on their childhood with some degree of angst. My home did not offer the security, acceptance, and guidance that parental love provides. My home was devoid of such blessings. As is typical in a severely dysfunctional family, there was just a lot of everything that shouldn't be in a home. There was always the endless barrage of verbal, physical, emotional, and mental abuse. Only years later did I recognize the sexual abuse that had also occurred. Or maybe it was only as an adult, after years of psychotherapy, that my mind could bear to admit it.

There was no respect in our home; no feelings of family connectedness. I felt no sense of worth as a child, no sense of pride or dignity. Our parents were insensitive to each other and rarely spoke civilly to us. In turn, we were intolerant of each other and could not carry on meaningful conversations. There were few stories or happy feelings shared—so little of the love, the trust, the caring found in a normal home. Respect? Love? Who knew what they were? Sarcasm, bickering, and rudeness reigned. If we held out our hands in need, they were filled with emptiness. That was the way life was lived in our house. That was our reality.

We had no positive role models: no guidance, no encouragement, no support system. There was little structure to our days and no meaningful discipline. Instead, we were chastised and humiliated over and over again. It was a hostile environment for a sensitive child, indeed for anyone. We were each lost in our own little hell, wrought by our responses to our genetics, environment, and toxic upbringing.

As I've navigated the journey of writing this, I've asked my siblings for verification. Am I exaggerating? Was I just too sensitive? Am I being melodramatic? No, I assure you. I know no words strong enough to describe that which lies beyond description—beyond explanation—my childhood and the effect it had on me while living it. Especially while living it. I had no words, only tears. Crying was something I became good at. It was a part of me for so many years.

Very early on in childhood I built a wall around myself an invisible barrier. I didn't have a name for it but later learned it was called "depression." It protected me from a harsh world when I could no longer deal with it—such pain, such anguish—so little hope of deliverance. My childhood, from where my problems stemmed, read like the anatomy of the deep-seated depression I was destined to live.

CHAPTER 13

Escapes

I got to an age when I would get up early before the noise and chaos began. I would start the fire in the kitchen stove and, in the winter, in the painfully cold room, I would sit with my coat on and my feet on the oven door. I'd heat some water, make some tea, and if the batteries in the radio weren't dead, I would quietly listen to country and western music. It wasn't usually the most uplifting music, but it was a distraction from the harsh reality around me. Whatever my thoughts were during those quiet times, they gave me a sense of peace That early morning silence helped keep me sane.

When the rest of the family got up, I could escape to the stables for a while and milk my cow. I would always put on a greyish brown adult trench coat over whatever else I wore, so I could remove it afterwards and rid myself of the smell of cow manure. The smell of the barn would leave me exposed to the embarrassing ridicule of certain classmates and this would cause me further trauma. I went to great lengths to avoid the humiliation—I already carried more than my share of shame.

It was during this time that I stopped drinking milk. Too often, it tasted of manure, no matter how careful I was while milking.

As time went by, I found outside escapes for myself. I had my favourite maple trees and my favourite season was autumn, as that's when my birthday was. And every year, the trees, my faithful friends, remembered me. They would shed their leaves and spread out, for me, my birthday gift, a crimson carpet, which spoke to me in rustles as I walked or lay upon the ground to dream. Every birthday, without fail, this gift was given to me. It was the only gift that I could count on. Maybe, just maybe, it was enough.

Always fearing ridicule, I never vocalized those dreams of mine, those innocent childish dreams. That would have been oh so foolish. It was as if I knew deep down that, in my world, they were impossible. Perhaps, truth lived within my child's heart of hearts because they were dreams only a child might dream in a land of nothingness

Nature was my refuge. In my desperate need, it was a friend who showed me beauty and grandeur beyond the confines of my home. It was inspiring. It resonated with my soul and gave me a sense of stability, continuity, and peace. I always knew that I would find what I needed there. It would not betray me.

I had my secret places beneath the evergreen trees where boughs came down to touch the ground to shield me and hide me from the world. I removed the shrubs and cleared the spaces as if it were my very own home. I'd make it neat and tidy. This place was my haven. In my own way, I did play, I just happened to be alone. And even as I played, I cleaned.

I didn't realize, at the time, what it was that I was doing. It's only in hindsight that I see a desperate child struggling to control what she could not control.

CHAPTER 14

Nature

The heavens declare the glory of God;
the sky proclaims its builder's craft.
—Psalm 19.2

Mixed in with my earliest memories are feelings of love and oneness with nature. It wasn't something I named, it was something I experienced and lived. Today, I would call it prayer or meditation or perhaps contemplation. I grew up very close to nature. I rejoiced in it. Its splendor filled a need in me. It touched my heart. It fed my soul. It was part of my salvation. In my world of turmoil, its beauty gave me a sense of peace, of wonder, and eventually, a belief in something or someone greater than us all. I felt these feelings most in nature's serenity and in my solitude. That was as close to real happiness that I could come. It kept me sane. At what point I began to associate this with God, I cannot say. Perhaps I always did but didn't know it.

I watched in silent awe the breathtaking beauty and the majesty of the sunrise and sunset and marveled at the changing scenes before me. They were an endless sea of vibrantly moving colours. So much the same yet always different. These performances were for me. They were my own private viewings. Often, I acted not only as an appreciative audience but also an adjudicator as sometimes I critiqued the scenes. There were times when I felt my heart would burst and I'd be moved to tell God that, once again, he had outdone himself—that today's performance far exceeded yesterday's. So often, I'd tell him in appreciation, "You make me smile, oh God. You make me smile." And to myself, I'd often say, "If I could just capture this beauty and, somehow, hold it in my heart, life would be so wonderful." If I could hold it within me I would live the vision of something so heavenly, something beautiful—beautiful beyond words. And in my times of desolation, I could bring it out and view it. I could immerse myself in it like a child being baptized and I would forget all else.

Yes, God and beauty were all around me yet not all around. The sun would set and I'd leave my vantage point and go home where the stark reality would break my reverie.

That God who deigned to paint the skies in radiant rainbow hues never saw fit to paint my sad world happy—at least not for any significant length of time—no matter how much I prayed or cried.

Was mine a lesser God or was I, perhaps, just less deserving?

CHAPTER 15

Summer Work

Grades 7, 8, 9 and 10

The summer before my thirteenth birthday, I went to work for a retired couple in Algonquin Park. They were very amiable and kind, even though she had to teach me how to clean a bathroom, how to iron shirts, and how to set a table properly. She even had to teach me how to sweep the floor without sending dirt flying all over. She had obviously never swept dirt and sand like that in our summer kitchen—out the open door. She accepted me; she gave me a chance. She must have wondered at my ignorance, but I was too shy and embarrassed to explain that, at home, I had ironed a lot, but I had done so with heavy greyish-black irons that were heated on the wood stove and had a handle that snapped off and on. I had never seen an electric iron before. And since we didn't have a bathroom at home, I had never cleaned one. I had never seen a set of matching silverware, let alone put it on a table properly. I probably wasn't much better at preparing fruit and vegetables or helping to cook and bake. But I needed the money and I'm sure they knew that. I clearly remember my initial purchase—my first pair of pajamas.

All summer long, their grown children returned home with the grandchildren to visit for a few days or even weeks. The young grandchildren were treated with such love and respect. I didn't know that kids were allowed to speak to adults, or that they could even speak intelligently. I didn't know that a growing child needed to be listened to as part of their learning process. It was unlike anything I had experienced or even imagined. What stunned me the most was the way they would sit around the table after dinner and talk and talk. I didn't know people could have so much to say or be so polite to each other and be so happy. I'd go back to the boarding house where I stayed and cry, perhaps in envy. I dared not even dream this dream for myself.

The house I worked in was situated in a beautiful setting on a lake. I fell in love with the sound of the waves lapping against the shore, and the forlorn cry of the loon spoke to my lonely soul. As best I could, I lost myself in nature and reading. They had always been such a comfort to me and now they were a godsend.

I wasn't quite a teenager yet, but physically I could pass for a sixteen-year-old. I was terribly self-conscious and even ashamed of my body and ill at ease in it. I had not yet learned to accept my own sexuality and felt uncomfortable and insecure and was embarrassed easily. Bodily functions had always been made fun of—laughed at— by my older brothers. They were vulgar and shameful. Sexuality was shameful. I looked like the other girls who were two or three years older than me, however what they saw, was the outward image I portrayed to hide my lack of self-esteem and social skills. I strived to fit in, but I didn't even know it was proper etiquette to look people in the eye when talking to them. Perhaps I feared they might see the pain, the hurt, the hate within me. I gradually started using self-deprecating humour to hide my ignorance of all that I should have learned during those growing up years when depression held me captive in isolation.

That summer proved to be a learning experience and prepared me for future work.

The next three summers my friend and I worked at a lodge just outside of our home town. It had a main building, the kitchen and dining room, and lovely rustic cabins built along the lake. We did housekeeping and acted as waitresses at mealtime. By this time, I had learned a great deal about cleaning a house and serving meals and felt very comfortable doing so. What really intrigued me was the fireplace in each cabin. I'd wonder aloud if perhaps, someday, I too, might be able to stay in such luxury. To me, it seemed like just another childish dream and not a possible future reality.

School and Work

Grades 11, 12 and 13

By the time I reached grade ten, I had decided, or come to believe, that what separated me from the rest of the world was further education. And I was determined to get that education. I was convinced it was the key to a better life. Of course, my father's beliefs were different. He believed that I didn't deserve or need further education. To him, "girls just got married and had babies," preferably in that order. To me, the thought of perpetuating my mother's life was unbearable. I would feel this panic rise up within me at the very thought. I felt my hopes being trampled. I cried a lot, I prayed a lot, I lived in hope. Hope was all I had. To move onto grade eleven meant I would have to move away from home. How could I afford to continue? Who would pay for my room and board and tuition for the next three years? And even if I could manage all of that, I'd still only have grade thirteen and no career training. They were questions that caused me great anxiety.

The high school was in a larger town some sixty miles away, which to me may as well have been ten times as far. I had seldom been that far from home. The school offered grades eleven, twelve, and thirteen, the final three grades.

I applied and was accepted by an all girls' school run by the Sisters of St. Joseph. Because my grade ten marks were so good, they waived my tuition. This was a good beginning, since I still wasn't sure where my room and board money would come from, and I had very little myself.

September came, which meant not only adjusting to a new town, a new school, and new classmates, but for me, the very uncomfortable, but necessary, situation of living in a stranger's home. I had only stayed over at a friend's home once in my life, so this was unbelievably stressful. My brother was a year ahead of me at a boys' school in this same town. He had found a cheap home for me to stay at. It was with an older woman, with straggly grey hair. She walked with a cane but still lived in her own home. Her son didn't want her living alone, which is why I was allowed to stay there. I'm not sure I would have been of any help to her, let alone know what to do in an emergency. I still felt self-conscious even using the telephone.

The cost of room and board was cheap, but still, there were times when the money was overdue. She would stand there and listen as I phoned home in tears to check if the money was coming and when and why it was late. It was a traumatic experience which repeated itself month after month and added to my sense of helplessness.

The house was an older home. It had electricity and heat which to me were luxuries, especially during the winter. The only indoor plumbing was water in the kitchen sink, which was a step up from my home where it still had to be carried in. There was no bathroom, only an outhouse out back. I had a pee-pot under my bed for night time, which was very convenient. In fact, in winter, it was a necessity. But it caused me great embarrassment to bring it downstairs and carry it through the kitchen to take it to the outhouse to empty it.

I was seventeen years old. Bodily functions were still a source of angst and shame for me.

It took an enormous amount of time and energy to cope with all my subjects and to keep up my outward facade. Although no one had ever used the word "depressed" to describe me, I felt that I was somehow different from other people. I didn't recognize depression in myself and had never seen a doctor for this pain that coursed through me. Unbeknownst to me, my abilities were compromised. Depression can wreak havoc with the mind and the memory. My thinking was slow and my ability to retain what I read was hampered. I couldn't just read notes or paragraphs and remember or explain them. I had to read it over and over as if to memorize it. Learning, to me, was a weird process. To pass exams, I memorized, but did I remember it later? Sometimes, yes. Too often, no.

The school year was a constant struggle. Not only did I have to keep my depressive moods in check, but also the loneliness was beyond anything I had imagined, even worse than what I had experienced at home. There was the daily stress of an unbelievably heavy workload. Classes ran from eight-thirty until four, and there were always, hours of homework. There was a television in the house, but I never watched it. In fact, I rarely watched TV during all my high school years. I had too much homework to do each night. Most other students didn't have as much difficulty keeping up, but they weren't in my state of mind or as meticulous as I was. I got less work done in school and I couldn't go to sleep until my homework was finished to the best of my ability. I buried myself in my studies and strove for perfection. I could not fail; I couldn't afford to. That would be disastrous—a fate worse than death, in my mind. Education came at a price. Failure was not an option. I could not, in my wildest dreams, imagine getting a second chance. To think of this was akin to a nightmare.

Academically I belonged. I was an excellent student and I excelled in most every subject. This pleased my teachers because it brought up their school's ranking. But none of them knew the real me. They never saw the struggles going on within me. They did not see, *"me,"* or rather the lack of *"me."* On the other hand, I had no idea about the problems and life issues other pupils were going through. I never talked much about myself or my home life, so why would I expect them to share theirs with me? In fact, outside of the school setting, I seldom saw my classmates. I really did not fit in. If I walked home with others and they happened to stop, as girls are wont to do, I had no money for pop, and it felt awkward and embarrassing always having them pay for me.

The school gym was only used for the occasional meeting, so my only exercise was walking to and from school. I did not participate in extracurricular activities. There was no balance in my life, only classes, books, and endless studies. So many nights, I still cried myself to sleep. The lost and hurting, unloved child still lived within me.

When life got really overwhelming and fears of failure assailed me, I'd go home for a weekend. That was enough to motivate me to continue my studies no matter what. Anything—anything was better than home. To have my life repeat that cycle would be intolerable. The thought helped to renew my resolve. I would persevere. I would graduate. That was as far ahead as I dared to look.

Part way into the school year, my cousin, who lived in the same town as my school, contacted me. She was a year older than I was and a high school dropout. She had a full-time job at a restaurant and a steady boyfriend. Occasionally, I would hang out with them, but time didn't mean the same to them as it did to me. I was overly conscious of the time I needed for my studies. Nevertheless, I got talked into working a shift or two each weekend as a waitress at the restaurant where she worked. I liked the work and it helped get me "outside of myself" and forced me to be more social. Besides, it was nice to have some spending money. I could now afford a pop with the girls which, to me, seemed like a luxury.

The school year ended, and I went to work at a store in Algonquin Park. It was the ideal setting. Two teenagers working for the summer holidays, in the same vicinity, in one of the most beautiful parks in Ontario, and as it turned out, one of the most romantic. Was it chance, or was it destiny, that brought us together? We spent time together walking the nature trails, hand in hand; exploring and enjoying the beach and the lake shore; listening to the sound of the waves wash against the rocks and the cry of the loons echoing across the lake; and often, we would just sit and talk. He was accepting and understanding.

All too soon, the summer passed, and at its end, he said, "I love you." The frightened, previously unloved girl truthfully replied, "I don't know what love is." It was the first time, those words had been spoken to me, ever. I was sixteen. My future husband was seventeen.

My family and friends all called it "destiny." It took me much longer to realize it.

That fall, when I headed back to school, I had room and board with a widow and her teenage son and daughter. They treated me like one of the family. I was much more relaxed and involved, at least, by my standards. I helped them with their homework, and they taught me how to play badminton, and sometimes, I even went to the movies. This was a huge step forward for me. But the highlight of my week was a letter from my boyfriend and, of course, answering it. I took time from my studies for this, although I was, once again, taking ten subjects and struggling to keep up. In spite of having passed grade eleven, I had no confidence in my academic ability and still thought of the worst case scenario every time I wrote an exam. That way, no matter what happened, it was always better than what I had imagined.

When the end of the year came, I went back to work in the park and so did my boyfriend. I was still too ashamed to have him visit me at my home, even though I only lived three miles outside of town. One weekend, when he hitchhiked to town and called me from a telephone booth, I talked to him for awhile, then hung up and left him there, on a wet dreary night, to sleep in the phone booth. I had no idea how to cope with such a situation. My younger sister and her boyfriend found out what was happening and we went to town to pick him up. Unfortunately, we couldn't find him. He was still in the phone booth where he spent the night. I was still sorely out of touch with the real world and what people normally do in such circumstances. Eventually, that summer, he did get to visit me at home. To my relief, where and how I lived didn't concern him that much. He accepted it and was neither scandalized nor judgemental and he didn't "dump me" as I so feared he would. He wanted to know the "real me."

September came and I went back to school to complete grade thirteen and he went back to college. This year, I stayed with an aunt. She had one daughter still living at home who was a couple of years younger than me. We got along well and she still treats me like a sister. But to her dismay, I seldom watched TV or listened to Elvis—her idol. I had developed little appreciation for music through the years. This was my final year and I had to pass departmental exams in June. They were set by the government. Just the thought of the exams caused me great apprehension. Failure was not an option. I dedicated myself to daily mass, classes and homework. Even as I lived in hope, I feared failure. I catastrophized, as if preparing myself for "what if?" I wasn't aware of it at the time, but it kept me always on edge and wasting precious energy.

I passed all my exams in June and graduated. Now came the fateful question. "What do I do with my life?"

Our Lady's Missionaries

After successfully finishing high school, I was now at a crossroads in my life. I could borrow money and either go into nursing or go to Teacher's College like my sister and brother had done. But I couldn't visualize myself in either career. And I definitely didn't feel ready for marriage. I was still looking for certainty and perfection, and marriage didn't offer that to me. Instead, I leaned towards a religious vocation. The Sisters of St. Joseph had taught me for the last three years of high school and obviously made an impression on me. But I wanted more than just life in a convent as I visualized it. What appealed to me was missionary work. I found a newly formed missionary order, "Our Lady's Missionaries," the only English-speaking, exclusively missionary community of religious women in Canada. It seemed only fitting that I join their order. Since childhood I had a special devotion to the Blessed Virgin Mary. She meant so much to me and so often I invoked her help. It seemed I was always in need of something. Like my mother, I was always making novenas to Mary—praying for special intentions. At the time, I thought they were never answered, but now I realize that they were, because I am here.

Religious life resonated within me and touched my soul, especially the Holy Sacrifice of the Mass, the prayers and the meditation around which a religious life revolves. There were many other exercises of importance; the rosary, Holy Hour, visits to the chapel, retreats, spiritual reading, and even grand silence. There were also the more mundane activities such as cooking and cleaning and sewing the "habits" and making the rosaries which we'd wear once we became Novices in ten months. Also on our schedule were classes and study that covered such subjects as the liturgy, sacred Scripture, the Christian vows, dogmatic and moral theology, church history, and more. This was all part of our formation as a religious person.

The structured and meditative life of the convent appealed to my obsessive-compulsive personality. There was a time and a place for everything. That suited me. But I was not a team player. When we put on the play *Heidi*, I volunteered to build an imitation brick fireplace as a prop. I did this with little help; I really didn't want help. I took it upon myself to do such things as remove the shrubbery and vines from under the trees in the backyard, much like I did in the trees at home when I was a child. I could do this on my own during free time and thus avoid talking. Talking—which was a break from our usual silence—was something most everyone else, normal young women, waited for and enjoyed. I had to be doing something. I felt that I had nothing to talk about, nothing to contribute to conversations. It was as if I had no past life.

Interwoven throughout these many activities was recreation. Recreation was a new concept for me, some parts in which I had trouble participating. Yet I knew I had to try. In the summer, we played baseball and hiked, which I really enjoyed. During the winter months, we sometimes went tobogganing. But the cold and the wet evoked childhood feelings and memories and my natural responses were still hard to deal with. Occasionally, during the winter, we went to an arena and played our version of hockey. I was overly aggressive, much like I had to be when playing with my brothers at home. I hogged the puck. I could stick handle right through the whole team and most always score. I had no idea of sharing or being part of a team. I missed the whole point of the game. I had no understanding of the concept of teamwork. In these areas I was a very unlikely candidate for the religious life and especially missionary work.

Every once in awhile, we had "talent night" when the talented and the not-so-talented, like myself, provided impromptu entertainment. We had one Novice who could do an almost perfect imitation of the comedienne Carol Burnett. Needless to say, I didn't know who Carol Burnett was—so limited had been my TV viewing. There had been very little comedy in my life.

My emotions were very confused. For the most part, my outward facade was impeccable. Yet there were times when I laughed and ended up crying. It was as Kahlil Gibran, the poet who said, "And the selfsame well from which your laughter rises was often times filled with your tears." In spite of all the tears I had shed, my well was still filled with tears. That wounded, helpless child still lived within me and those age old feelings of nothingness and worthlessness had not yet healed.

For two-and-a-half years I remained a member of Our Lady's Missionaries. I wore their habit. I loved and lived their rule, their way of life. It was hard to accept that I did not have a religious vocation. The desire was there but not the gift. To God "who had known and loved me before I was formed in the womb," I could not surrender myself. I did not know myself. I still had not developed a sense of self or self-identity. There was still no *"me."* I could not give what I did not have.

Yet the years I spent in the convent were as much a part of my formation as a person as were my years of high school. They were part of my salvation. I was not ready for the outside world yet, and these years gave me the time and opportunities for emotional and spiritual growth.

I had been overly idealistic in my vocational discernment and lacked a mature, realistic view of religious life. Other than the desire to do something useful with my life, to have it count for something, I had not looked in depth at what being a missionary entailed. What would happen after I made vows, what work I would train for, or what country I might be sent to work in.

I didn't realize that the religious, living in a convent, are like a family living in a house. They are united in love for God and for each other. I was still a girl questioning, "What is love?"

During my last days in the convent, the future looked scary and bleak to me. But it was my future and, even in my confusion, I knew that the experience of the years just past had put into my hands the very instruments with which I would carve my destiny.

My Career through the Years

After leaving the convent, I became a weekend Catholic. I attended mass on Sundays and fulfilled other obligations, but as a secular, God and religion were assigned second place. I seldom talked about that part of my past life. And yet, at that time, I thought nothing would ever replace it. I had no idea what my mission in the outside world would be; a world I had not easily fit into before and which now seemed to be a constant challenge. I still wore my mask to cover my apprehension. The childhood feelings had not abated.

I went to work as a bookkeeper for Ontario Hydro at a project in a remote location, accessible only by train. I loved the work. I was slow and meticulous, but I was accurate, something bookkeeping demands. I made a couple of friends and started to realize that I was not unique in my sufferings. I recognized it in my co-workers as well.

My boyfriend graduated from University and we got engaged. Within the year we were married. We had known each other for six years and had kept in touch, so this didn't surprise anyone. It was exciting yet frightening, surreal even. I still had my fears: I was searching for certainty, for Hollywood's "happily ever after." I had little idea of what constituted a mature, healthy marriage. I had never witnessed one that could have been considered "normal." And I was desperately lacking a sense of "self" so it was difficult for me to have an adult-to-adult relationship.

The day came when I held my first son in my arms. I was granted what, to me, was a miracle. I was flooded with overwhelming feelings of maternal love beyond anything I had ever imagined. But even as I held my precious, vulnerable baby in my arms, I cried. How could I possibly take care of a baby? I could hardly take care of myself. I knew that, in some ways, especially emotionally, I was still a child. I felt so deficient and frightened.

A few years later, my second son was born. There were many good times—times when we were very happy and enjoyed life. I especially took pleasure in watching my sons grow. I was loving to the best of my ability; I just didn't realize that. In my fears, I prayed that, as a mother, I would be able to give my children what had not been given to me.

As always, in public, I put forth my façade of civility in hopes of concealing depression's shameful presence. Unfortunately, my family bore the brunt of its scourge: the crying, the cursing and sarcasm, the cutting criticism, the swearing, and especially the anger. There were other times when, in apathy and exhaustion, I withdrew, wanting only to lie down and sleep, and sleep, and cry, and sleep some more. Between bouts of severe depression, my emotions were all over the place. I would feel okay one day or one week and depressed the next. There were times when my husband didn't know if he'd come home to the same person he had said goodbye to in the morning. I tried to stop using the word "depressed" so often, when my son started saying he was so "pressed." It was heartbreaking. It was one of the first words he learned. He was absorbing the ugly parts of the life around him.

I frequented doctors' offices, however, there was little treatment, little belief in my illness. Doctors weren't sure what they were treating. For years, depression was not spoken about. It was not diagnosed; each of the symptoms were individually addressed. The usual choice of treatment for the anxiety and tears was tranquilizers. It was a trade-off. Ease the pain but suffer the consequences—the sedation effect. On top of it all were the endless headaches, all too often, migraines. There were times when I felt like a zombie. I'd spend days lying on the couch, vaguely conscious of what the boys were doing. I was blessed in that they were such good kids and no emergencies arose.

I did not know what I had to give to my young family. I did what I considered normal. When I wasn't in the depths of depression, meals were made, the house was kept clean, and the laundry was done. I strived to have structure, routine, and tidiness in our lives, since there had been none in mine. Towels were kept clean, and always folded lengthwise, and hung on the rack the same way. Every shirt was ironed and put on a hanger facing to the right with the collar buttoned up. Besides shirts, I conscientiously ironed almost everything: my bras and panties, my husband's work pants and undershirts, the sheets and pillowcases, even the boys' clothes. Holidays, like Christmas, were especially stressful. I'd push myself—overwhelm myself—with all that I wanted to get done. Wasn't this my job? But I knew I was somehow "different." My friends didn't need to spend all day in the house but my work never seemed to be finished.

I was still unsure as to what I wanted to do in the future, so during those early years of marriage and motherhood, I took some university courses by correspondence and night classes—English, history and sociology. I loved English most of all and immersed myself in it. I was enthralled with the written word and loved poetry. It has such beauty. It fed my soul and kept my mind occupied. It extended from the mundane to the spiritual. For a year, I had a steady diet of indulging in English studies, morning, noon, and night. I knew I was over doing it when, one day, I found my two-and-a-half-year old sitting on the vacuum cleaner in the broom closet, with the door closed. He was "reading a book." I then turned my attention to sewing, for which I found I had a natural ability. I lost myself in it. I sewed for myself, the boys, my sister and her daughters, and others. It was a productive period in my life. I was probably as happy as it was possible for me to be at that time.

When my sons got a little older, I attended adult education courses to prepare myself for office work. I found the subjects interesting and was ready to embark on my first job when we made the decision to move from Ontario to Alberta. Settling in was difficult for all of us. To begin with, I wasn't much help. I hate change and don't adjust easily; I cried a lot. I'd unpack a box, then go back to bed and cry some more. This kept repeating itself. I was of little support to the rest of the family. My husband became very busy with a new company and a new job. The boys went everywhere together mostly for moral support. Our neighbours were wonderful, but again I was struggling with a deep depression.

For many years, after my sons were in school full time, I did bookkeeping for various companies. It suited me best when I worked by myself and was paid a salary for the job and not by the hour. That way I could spend as much time as I needed to do the work to the best of my ability, and not worry about overtime charges. I loved office work. Bookkeeping and accounting can be like a giant jigsaw puzzle. I knew what to do and did it. Weekdays could be hectic, stressful, and demanding. But it was the weekends that were a bigger problem. I had to make choices, mundane choices, yet difficult ones for me to make. I felt like I was never caught up. I would procrastinate, get more stressed out and less able to cope. I claimed I was "allergic to weekends."

As the years passed, I participated in a number of organizations: the Parent Teachers' Association, the Catholic Women's League, and the Hospital Auxiliary. The notion of recreation came to me gradually through my friends. At different times in my life, I played badminton, I bowled, and I curled. I even tried aquacise, yoga, and aerobics. Outwardly, I lived a rather normal life. I always dressed appropriately, by my own standards. Often, I was overdressed because when I looked at others, I saw perfection; that was how the outside world looked to me. I saw myself as flawed and tried to compensate. My family portrayed what I desired: a normal, happy, young family.

Underneath it all, depression lived and often bared its frightful fangs.

Time passed. When a lay counseling course was offered in town, I became a volunteer lay counselor and worked as one for quite a few years. This had a positive effect on my mind. Later on, I did volunteer work at a school reading with grade two students. It was rewarding to see their progress through the year. In fact, I'm certain their pronunciation was sometimes better than mine.

Nuances, Manners and Maturity

I never really learned the nuances of a poised, mature adult. Such subtleties are often age-appropriate, and if not learned during those certain windows of opportunity, they are hard to come by later. For me, their development was greatly thwarted. Growing up as a destitute, depressed individual, such opportunities if recognized, were considered mostly insignificant. Survival was uppermost in my mind.

Through the years, most women develop their own distinctive tastes. They might enjoy Royal Doulton dishes, Swarovski crystal, lace tablecloths, and Oneida silverware. I never developed such tastes. I never had the time for such luxury; I was too busy fighting depression, and my mind was conditioned by poverty. I settled for the essentials. I chose durability, affordability, and practicality.

I had no finesse, no grace, and was often too blunt, and then felt that I should apologize; but I had never learned how to apologize and I felt awkward to even attempt it. In all my life, no one had ever apologized to me.

During the years, when I volunteered with a grade two class at our local school, one of these seven-year-old students told me something that I found most enlightening. She said her mother told her to make sure her mind was in gear before opening her mouth. I felt as if she was speaking directly to me. Growing up I had no one to tell me such things gently, tactfully. I would have been told, rudely, to "Keep my mouth shut." There had been no one to teach me manners or the niceties of life. It was only after leaving home that I acquired some skill, and even then, I was still grossly lacking. Sometimes I felt too shy to even say, "Thank you." It felt unnatural and embarrassing for me. It definitely was not part of the language we used at home and rarely had anyone ever said, "Thank you," to me.

Nothing in my life was age-appropriate. From childhood, I developed sporadically between bouts of depression. In later years, as I raised my two sons, I also grew as they grew. But because of the obstacles to my personal growth, I must honestly admit that my sons reached maturity before I did.

At times I can still react inappropriately, as my family and friends can attest. I envy people who are calm, composed, and dignified, and who respond appropriately, whatever the problem or the occasion while I am bouncing off the walls. I now believe that if I were to ask God to change something, He wouldn't change me; He would take down the walls!

PART
2

Searching for Sanity

Depression

There have been countless articles and books written on the subject of depression—the causes, its signs and symptoms, and also the available treatments.

Researchers believe that depression involves a chemical imbalance in the areas of the brain that regulate mood and emotion. In depression, two key messengers—serotonin and noradrenaline—have irregularities which cause a malfunction of the central nervous system. Depression is anything but trivial. It is a common yet profound emotional illness. According to the World Health Organization major depression is a leading cause of death and disability worldwide. Every year, approximately one million people die by suicide around the world. This means nearly one life is lost to suicide every forty seconds.

Depression is an insidious disease. It attacks the very essence of a person. It is but one form of mental illness and it is the most treatable. Depression does not discriminate. It has no regard for who you are or what you have. Depression can affect anyone regardless of age, sex, race, social class, or religion. Some very famous and successful people in history have suffered from depression, including: Abraham

Lincoln, Winston Churchill, Michelangelo, and Princess Diana, to name a few.

Depression is not something "out there" that can be seen. It lies within us. No one is immune. Everyone in their lifetime, directly or indirectly, will be impacted in some way by mental illness; either themselves, a family member, a loved one, a friend, or co-worker. Almost twenty percent of the population will experience a diagnosable mental illness.

Depression has nothing to do with a weakness in one's character or personality. Everyone experiences "highs" and "lows" in life, but people with mood disorders experience them with greater intensity and for longer periods of time. When symptoms last for two weeks or more, and they are so severe as to interfere with daily living, it is called depression. Depression is a real illness, a serious illness, and cannot be cured by simply thinking positively. It can range from a bad case of the blues to a debilitating condition that can render a person incapacitated, languishing in a psychiatric ward, oblivious to themselves and those around them.

The signs and symptoms of depression are many and varied and are often misdiagnosed. It affects eating habits, sleep, self-esteem, memory, and concentration. Even the simplest decision can be impossible. Lethargy plagues the person and prevents them from living productively and this adds to the depression. To socialize can be almost impossible. Interest in life itself is lacking and hopelessness rules.

Depression is not simple. It is a life-threatening illness. It can overwhelm the personality with feelings of sorrow, guilt, shame, and self-loathing. In some cases, the "self" can shrivel up and disappear and the depressed person becomes an "invisible person." Depression ravishes the mind and sickens the body. It kills the spirit, robbing it of all that is worth feeling good about. For the most part, those who suffer from depression seek to protect themselves from disclosure for fear of ridicule.

Depression wreaks havoc on a person's life and the lives of everyone around them. It can confuse, anger, and alienate family, relatives, and friends. The depressed person can change into a stranger and be difficult or impossible to be around. They feel that everyone else around them has changed. They don't realize that it is they who have changed. This adds to their experience of loneliness. Those who try to help them feel just as cut off and lonely as those suffering from the condition.

Love is depression's most powerful enemy. But love alone cannot control or cure it. And not everyone is blessed or lucky enough to experience the much needed love. To recover from a serious depression, a person needs medication—antidepressants—to manage the chemical imbalance, and the invaluable help of psychological therapy. Sometimes electroconvulsive treatments may even be necessary. A positive mental attitude, support groups, or even going to church can also be helpful.

Effects of Depression

Research shows that childhood trauma leaves imprints on a child's brain. Significant abuse can indelibly mark and alter genes in its young victims. This, in turn, affects their physical, mental, and emotional development, leaving them less able to deal with challenges and stress later on in life.

Abuse takes many forms such as criticism, threats, accusations, and humiliation. Being yelled at, as I so often did with my sons, can violate a person's sense of self. It belittles them. From experience, and from observing my brothers and sisters through the years, I would say that abuse also leaves its mark upon the heart and the soul. These "imprints" are invisible, but I know that they are there. I have felt and lived them. I have known the trauma and borne the scars that a dysfunctional childhood inflicts. As a parent who had suffered such abuse as a child, I should have known the pain and the harm I was causing my sons. And yet I did not act accordingly. I was too engrossed in fighting my own inner battles.

Throughout my sons' childhood years my mood swings came often and they were unpredictable. Often I was "touchy," short-tempered, and "headachy" as I tried to manage my persistent migraines. Worst of all was the anger that burned deep within me. It could erupt explosively at the least provocation—or sometimes with no provocation—and life for my family would become insufferable. I'd push them away with my sarcasm and even my silence. They had experienced this all too often. They were helpless and trapped. They knew it would end; they just weren't sure when—and neither was I. During these episodes everyone in the house was subdued. They tolerated me, and swallowed their hurt, their pain, and fears, and would try to avoid me, even leaving the house, if possible. My oldest son had his books, My younger son had his friends, My husband had his sports. These were their coping mechanisms. What did I have? Nothing except my depressions.

During these times I struggled immensely just to cope. Getting up in the morning and staying up was a luxury of which I did not partake. Sometimes I managed to do bare essentials. Some days I did nothing. Life went on, and my family managed as best they could without me. I was incapable of meaningful interaction with any of them. Interactions would become battles and I didn't want to fight.

The pain, the anguish, that depression wreaks on the individual and the people in their lives who love and care for them is incalculable. I quote from my 1981 journal entry. "I'm so tired and so confused—just let me lie down and sleep. I don't want to go through another three months like the past ones. I don't think I have the energy. It's not worth it… There's Murray saying we can't talk when you're yelling…and Jeff crying inside because I get so angry at Murray, and he questions whether I love Daddy. It doesn't sound like it at times; and what would he like to see changed, change the mopey feeling—you don't want to get up and do anything and then, when you do get up, you're mad because of what you didn't do. And then there's Paul suggesting that if I'm going to change anything, I should change how fast and how often I get angry and sarcastic and nag, nag, nag. I feel as if I'm losing them all right now and the idea of doing things differently is impossible because I'm so controlled by this hellish turmoil inside of me. I get to the point where I swear I won't open my mouth again. It seems that everything I say is wrong."

Being a mother didn't end my perfectionism. I still felt I had to deal with all the probabilities and possibilities of life, not just for myself but for everyone. Maybe it was the need for control or perhaps it was the sense of responsibility ingrained in me to look after others. I felt that my sons' neatness, cleanliness, and manners, or lack of, reflected on me—on the illusion of perfection I held. So many of my fears and limitations I imposed on them.

Deeply rooted in my mind were many erroneous beliefs from childhood. Probably the worst belief was that a parent was responsible for shaping their children, even if that meant disciplining them with anything I could get my hands on. This, I did occasionally in my fits of anger. I cringe in shame when I think about it. My sons were as perfect as two boys possibly could be. Yet I passed on to them what I had learned from my parents—toxic discipline, toxic behavior. It makes me cry, and I pray that I've been forgiven.

This I remember; this I will never forget. I have vivid memories of the fear in my children's eyes and the heartbreak of knowing that it was I, a parent, who put it there. I remember the pain of seeing my son crying and feeling the hurt I was causing him because I couldn't cope at home and had to go back into the hospital, again and again. Reminiscent of my childhood are the simple pleasures I denied them. I regret such things as not letting them build a tree house in the bush out of sight of the house when they and their friends were so excited about their plans. So often, I squashed their fun, their adventurous spirit.

I know what it's like to fly into a rage because my son didn't think it was a problem to postpone a meal when he was out of town at a basketball game. Those feelings of childhood unworthiness, of deserving nothing, of being insignificant—that "nothingness" swept over me in an overwhelming flashback. My anger burst forth out of control. I had just brought the week's groceries into the house and, like a child, having a temper tantrum, I started throwing the groceries around the kitchen. I threw and broke a bottle of Scope against the cupboard door, it put a crack in the door and sprayed mouthwash around the room. That brought me back to my senses. My son was the adult in the room, not I. He knew that missing, or postponing, a meal was no big deal. I didn't want my children to experience the feelings of unworthiness that I had felt so strongly as I grew up. But

I went about it all wrong and I still didn't understand enough to explain my actions or where my feelings came from. I had never heard of "flashbacks."

I know what it's like to push family to the breaking point. To break hearts, to break spirits, and to have too much fear and shame and pride to ask for forgiveness, regardless of the pain I have caused. Sometimes, there was the awful pain of survival itself. In my journal I note, "I am in survival mode—I have been for days—or has it been weeks? Time doesn't matter. Time doesn't exist. I exist; but I wish I didn't. I've been thrown into this hellish abyss. I can no longer cope. I can no longer fight. Every day repeats itself: I get up and I go back to bed over and over and over again. Insanity? The pain is excruciating. I curl up in a fetal position and vegetate. I do not live. I do not die. I merely survive; I exist."

Whenever I came out of an episode of depression, I would always have these awful, overwhelming feelings of guilt and shame. I would feel so sheepish, so embarrassed by my behavior. I could not explain it to my family, or even understand myself, what had gone on within my head. It always surprised me that my family were still the same when I believed they had changed somehow. It took a long time before I realized, and accepted, that it was I who had temporarily changed. I was the one who switched from love to hate and back again. I wondered, and questioned, which one was the real me—the one who loved or the one who hated? I had been both for so long. Only time gave me the reasons and the answers for which I searched.

CHAPTER 22

Depression Can Be Fatal

I feel this crushing need but I know not what for. This need I feel in every fiber of my body. It's unrelenting and it screams from my very core. It screams to be heard, to be understood, to be dealt with. This overwhelming desperate need that lies within me also lies beyond me. Is it a similar need that drives the alcoholic to drink, the addict to do drugs, me to escape?

There were times when I'd escape the only way I knew how. Enabled by pills that tranquilize, I'd sleep, I'd wake, I'd tranquilize, and again, I'd sleep. And so the vicious cycle of numbing the pain of reality, of depression, would go on and on. I knew what to take and what not to take. I knew how much to take, and no more. This too, they won't let me do in the hospital, so leave me out. They won't let me sleep that self-drugged sleep of escape. Yet, somewhere in my pain-crazed mind, irrationally, I'd rationalize, "I can't kill myself if I'm asleep."

Some say suicide is an "easy out." I disagree vehemently. There's nothing easy about taking your own life. That happens at the end of a struggle in which a person feels they have exhausted all options available to them, when there is no light only the darkness of abject despair. A mind in that stage is beyond analysis, beyond understanding, beyond rational thought and decision making. If I had conscious thought I believe my decision would be to live even though assailed by the traumatic feelings of despair. A human's inherent instinct is to live.

I know what it's like to wish you were dead, when life just doesn't seem to be worth living. I know what it's like to be alive yet not living, when life is devoid of hope, of joy and meaning, when the pain of living feels insurmountable. There have been times when I didn't want to live, but I didn't want to kill myself either. I feared hell, but I didn't fear death. I feared suicide as a cause of death. I have lived the pain of those feelings from hell that made me want suicide to be an option, although I knew it never was because my Roman Catholic upbringing is so ingrained in me. As well, my conscience had been formed by belief in a fearful, yet merciful and loving God. I remembered what I'd been taught: "Suicide, when the conscience, where man is alone with God, is no longer working and God's voice cannot be heard in this secret sanctuary in man's depth."

And yet, there were times when I could live only because I knew that I could die if I so chose. But, miraculously, that was an option I never chose. I had my cache of pills, and I knew some combinations that were lethal. It was hard to give them up when I finally did. They were my security blanket. I no longer have a need for them. I have grown past those feelings of hopelessness that come before despair, those feelings of long ago, and yet not so long ago, when I felt that there was nothing I could do and that there was no one to help me.

I have learned when and where and how to seek help; shame no longer guides me.

The Puzzle

I have been in the local hospital for a short time and am well enough now for an afternoon pass to go home and see how well I can cope. It is a beautiful day and it's only a short way to go, so I walk.

I am on 47th street, about halfway home, when a giant jigsaw puzzle appears on the sidewalk before me. It is there briefly; just long enough for me to recognize that it is a picture of my life. A picture of my life in its totality. And every piece fits perfectly. That is what strikes me the most. Somewhere, somehow the chaos of my life makes sense. This is a consoling revelation to me. I am not alone. Someone or something is masterminding the pieces of my life; I'm merely living them.

At this point in my depression, I took this snapshot of the completed puzzle as a sign of recovery—of the possibility of wholeness. But my actual recovery, the point at which I could honestly say, "my mind is not sick anymore" would not come for another fifteen years. And so I clung to every glimmer of hope that came my way and this was one of them.

Life went on.

CHAPTER 24

Screams

My soul be still and wait without hope,
for hope would be for the wrong thing.
—T. S. Eliot

If I had hope, what would I hope for? It's another time, another encounter with the enemy. There have been so many in my lifetime. Those demons who live within me, I know they never leave, they only sleep; and now they've been awakened. Once again, I have been rendered useless, hopeless. I crawl into bed and curl up in a fetal position and sleep. I sleep a lot, whenever I am so lucky. I cry incessantly. Reality is proving too much for me. I've retreated behind my wall of depression. I'm now in survival mode; I have been for weeks, or has it been months? I wouldn't know; I've lost all sense of time. Sometimes, I hear vague noises of life, of everyday living, but I'm not part of it. Life is suspended. My pain is amplified. I know what it feels like when even God is in question. When it feels that all around you and within you are enemies screaming degrading taunts.

When I can, I rise. I'm extremely agitated as I sit on the edge of my bed. Deep and hellish sobs rack my body. Laying down intensifies the pain; it's unbearable. To stand is nigh impossible. My legs give way. My knees buckle. I try to walk, I stagger like a drunkard; I fall and so I sit where I have landed, bent forward, I hug myself, and in rhythm with my sobs, I rock like a mother consoling a crying child. But there are no loving mother's arms to hold me. In all my life, there have never been. I am now in the arms of depression: cold, loveless, unwielding arms. I have regressed. I am a child again. A desperate hurt child who doesn't know how to cope, to fight, to live. I am too small, too young. This is beyond my understanding. I do not have the presence of mind to tell myself, "This too shall pass." It wouldn't matter. I would never believe it anyway.

Nearing exhaustion, I slide to my knees and smother my face in the bedding between my outstretched arms. I hear screams. They go on and on. Whose screams are they? They engulf me. Am I possessed? Are they my screams? I cannot tell. Why is there screaming? I don't understand. I just know there is, and I know that they are screams of desperation.

When I first viewed the famous painting "The Scream" by Edvard Munch, I felt an instant connection. He captured the essence of my primeval pain—the anguish of my depressions. I have felt that scream in every fiber of my body. Over and over, I have screamed that scream. But there's been no one there to paint me in my despair. And my pain, my scream is not a static picture on the wall of some museum.

Splinters

I am back in the hospital. I have had a relapse. I had asked my doctor to admit me. It is safe here. They have me on suicide watch. They don't tell me this, but I know. I've been here before in this same room right across from the nurse's station.

This episode, like so many others, built up like a storm within me. Gradually, then more aggressively, the dreaded darkness took over my mind. And then I felt as if some internal explosion shattered my mind into so many splinters. I feel the splinters and then the pain. I liken it to nails piercing flesh and splintering the wood of a cross on a hill so long ago. I cry; I try to pray to Him who is not listening. I am so very tired. I sleep a lot—a drugged restless sleep. But mostly, I wait. I wait for what, for the pills to work their magic, for time to ease the pain, for God to work a miracle?

This mind of mine, it is *not* mine. It cannot tell me.

As sick as I am, somehow I know that all these splinters must come together, be glued together, become one—only then will I feel well again.

My words are few, but when I say the word *depression*, these doctors and nurses, they cannot feel what I'm feeling—they cannot feel my pain and the turmoil, the confusion, and the fears. Most especially, they cannot hear the screams echoing in my head from this deep, dark place where I am at. If only I could show them. If only I could tell them what's in my head, in my mind. If only they could see and feel. If only they could understand.

Once again I have retreated behind my wall of silence, into the void of depression. This is my world and I keep it secure. Behind my wall is what they're looking for. They are looking for me.

I ask my doctor, "Will I ever get out of here?" He answers simply, "Yes." He does not explain to me how or why he knows, but I cling to his words. They speak to me of hope, and hope is what I need the most right now. It's all I've got.

Dr. Kenneth

Do No Harm
—Hippocratic Oath

Finally, a psychiatrist is coming to my town twice a month. I thought I was one of the lucky ones. I was working at the medical clinic at the time. To the bewilderment of my family doctor, I asked to be one of the new psychiatrist's first patients. I had waited so long for this to happen. I had hoped and prayed for years for a mental health professional to deal with my depression.

Shortly into this first appointment, I am crying. The psychiatrist's sarcasm is so unexpected, so cutting, and so unprofessional. I am completely taken aback. It's as if I've been forcefully slapped in the face. Dr. Kenneth is everything a doctor shouldn't be. He is the most sarcastic son-of-a-bitch I have ever met, unbelievably sarcastic, relentlessly sarcastic. I had lived with sarcasm all of my life. I couldn't stand it then and I can't stand it now.

He does not believe that I am depressed; he thinks it's all an act, a charade, I'm just pretending. After all, I'm leading a normal life. I'm looking after a home and family; I am holding down a job, and in spite of my tears, I can converse intelligently with him. So why do I consider myself depressed?

I don't fit the psychiatric profile of a depressed person. I don't fit into their books! How could I fit into their books? How could I conform to their idea of what a depressed person was like? I had not evolved from a book. Since childhood, I had lived with depression—beyond depression. I was depression and depression was me. And yet, in his eyes, I am a fraud.

I had learned to mask my depression so successfully and the fact that I was able to function in a seemingly normal manner was now proving to be a great disadvantage to me and to my treatment in the mental health system. I was living a charade but not in the way he accused me; this was the only way I knew how to live. It was part of my survival technique. I had lived this way all of my life. For me, it was normal.

He keeps questioning sarcastically. "You want someone to take care of you?" I do not respond, but if I could, I would tell him the folly of his question. But I have no voice. Is it shame that prevents me from admitting to him that even as a child I looked after myself? There was no one there to care for me. I do not need to be looked after as he so scathingly put it. I need to be heard. But childhood emotions have been evoked. They rise to the surface and overwhelm me. I keep crying. His questions cut me to my very core. Some are questions that are too personal to even attempt to answer.

He opens wounds that are traumatic and memories that are like reliving childhood. I have always tried to keep those scars well-covered, but he is callous, insensitive to my feelings.

I have always been a very guarded person. I had never talked to anyone, not even my husband, about my early life—about the hurt, the suicidal and depressing thoughts and feelings I had kept hidden so deep inside. How could I admit them to this man, a stranger? How could I trust him? As part of the outside world he was an enemy.

I cannot tell him my secrets. How can I expose my past—a time of such abuse—a time devoid of love and hope and normality? How can I reveal the feelings of sinfulness and shame that have haunted me? I found it all so degrading.

I thought that my family's way of life was unique—that no one else had felt my feelings of ugliness, poverty and isolation.

My past was shrouded in toxic shame. Besides, how could this psychiatrist possibly fathom a person, in this day and age, in this country, still being raised in third-world conditions? And I can't tell him. I find it all too painfully humiliating. I have a desperate need for healing, but my shame is greater. My pain is intense, but my fear wins out—fear that he might find me out, fear that he might see that beneath my masks I am a "nothingness." With my complete lack of self-esteem and my feelings of worthlessness, how could I handle that?

I hurt indescribably and for this doctor to deny my hurt, my depression, was devastating. I cannot think, I cannot process this chaos. I have no words, only tears, and they are being judged as childish—as a cover-up and not as a symptom of my illness, my depression.

Depression, like all mental illness, still carried a damning stigma. But even the stigma had not deterred me. I had actively sought help, but now, where was the empathy and support I had expected, that I needed? This encounter was as unpredictable and chaotic as my childhood had been.

At home, my husband doesn't understand where all my tears, turmoil, and rage are coming from. He finds it hard to believe that any doctor can be as sarcastic as I claim. My husband accompanies me to one of my appointments and he hears for himself what I found so hard to describe. He also witnesses for himself my painful and caustic interaction with this psychiatrist. He agrees with me that this doctor's attitude and his sarcastic approach are unacceptable and he wants me to stop seeing him. He questions why I want to keep going back and he points out that, at home, after each session, I regurgitate all that had been said and how it had been said. It was an ongoing source of trauma and tears. Each morning, I would pull myself together and go to work for the day only to come home and cry some more, often hysterically.

With each appointment, the scene repeats itself. Like a self-fulfilling curse, the harassment continues. I dread each appointment but I can't give up. I hurt too much. I have suffered too long. I am so tired; I just want the pain to stop. In my own way, I could cope with the outside world, but most of the time, I was not really living; I was just existing. This psychiatrist was my only connection to the mental health system. As questionable as his approach was, he was the person, the professional, who was supposed to be able to help me. If my psychiatrist can't help me, who can?

In some perverse way, he was my hope, even as he trampled my hope on the floor before me.

By now, both my husband and I know that I should be hospitalized. But my psychiatrist refused to admit me. He said, "There was no place he could send me." If I were physically ill, he would "know where to send me." If I were depressed, he would "know where to send me." But in his opinion, I was neither sick nor depressed.

I made a big, bad mistake. I claimed that my psychiatrist was driving me to drink because I started adding Kahlua to my coffee. It calmed me. My husband, pointed out that before I started seeing this doctor I was not a drinker. The doctor picks up on this immediately. Now come his words of entrapment. Like a poisonous snake, sarcasm dripping with every word, he pounces on my words. "Now, if only I could make you an alcoholic, I would know where to send you." Incensed, my anger erupts, like a sleeping volcano awakening, and I throw the box of Kleenex at him. It was the only thing within my reach. Somewhere deep inside my mind, words of defiance form. "You crafty son-of-a-bitch." But the words remain unspoken drowned within my tears. To him, this was a victory. To me, it was an indication of just how devious his mind was and I didn't want to fall victim again. I had done my own research. I had read so many books as I searched for answers. I knew that no one could make me anything. It was up to me, I was responsible. But I remain speechless. His sly insinuations force me to hide. His tactics make me fearful. A deeply rooted instinct rises up within me and I disappear behind my wall of anger. He cannot reach me here. But I dare not tell him this. He would deride me. He would twist my words and throw them back in my face.

As fate would have it, I have been crying throughout the session and I needed more tissue and I had to walk across the floor to retrieve the box from where it had landed at his feet. It felt so belittling, so demeaning. If I had this to do over again, I would not give him such satisfaction. I would wipe my nose on my sleeve.

At home, I cursed on a lot, I swore a lot; I screamed and pounded a lot of things. I cried incessantly. My psychiatrist was driving me crazy—or crazier—as the case might be. Inside me, a war was raging. It was as though a demon was screaming to come out. Is this what it feels like to lose your mind? Do you actually hear and feel it crack? Does that lessen the pain? Does that take the pain away? If so, dear God, let me hear my mind crack. Let this pain go away.

In desperation, I go to my family doctor. Needless to say, he sides with the psychiatrist. He points out that this doctor comes with impressive credentials. So who am I to question him? Then he adds a short puzzling statement regarding the psychiatrist. He says "He knows you."

How could he possibly know me? He can't or doesn't even talk to me in a civil manner. He sits there in all his pompous superiority and harasses me, but he does not know me. He drives the real Diane into hiding, deep within, barricaded behind a wall of distrust and fear, of hurt and anger.

And what are credentials—just words, printed words, on a framed piece of paper hanging on the wall. What matters is how those words are executed!

But they were the doctors. They had the power. They were in charge. They were the professionals. I was merely a patient, a pawn in their hands.

I am depressed and I know I'm depressed; I have been for a very long time. Nothing can negate the reality of my depression. But with this psychiatrist's attitude and his approach to treatment, there's no way he'll ever believe me. He doesn't want my diagnosis. He wants to make his own. He makes no attempt to see me as I am—to accept and to understand me. To do so would be beneath him. He would have to relinquish some of his power, some of his beliefs.

Sometimes, during our sessions, I was asked where my responsibility in all of this was. Where was my power as a person? "What power?" my mind questions. I could not explain to him that I felt no personal power. How could I? I am not yet a person. I have not yet learned to value myself—to accept myself as having some importance in this world. I am a "non-person"; I have no worth. This I learned as a child. I am a "nothingness."

His approach remains calculated and as cutting as usual. It's more than I can handle. I hear his words. I feel their sting. My tears continue. But he does not see the hurting child who sits in tears before him and I cannot tell him why I'm crying. What was there to tell? I had cried all my life. It was as much a part of me as breathing. How could I explain my tears? They defied description. These tears spoke volumes, but he could not understand this language I was speaking.

I swear he aimed to break me; which he did mentally, emotionally, physically. Like a crystal vase, falling in slow motion until its crash upon the floor, I am broken. My life lies there, like so many broken jagged pieces. I am desperate, but I am resilient beyond even my own belief. I am a survivor. I cry, I pray. Sheer stubbornness and hope keep me fighting. I have been trapped in this prison called depression for far too long. No one should have to live carrying hell within them. This is not normal. I know that my constant struggle to function is not normal. I know that, underneath the many masks I wear, I am quite literally coming undone.

For one of the few times in my life, I have the courage to defy authority. But I do not have enough courage, to confront him in person. I'm too fearful, I'm too beaten down, I am too emotional. He is a tower of strength, and he is against me, his patient. I know I am no match for him. He is too forceful and cunning, and I might be intimidated and back down, I can't let that happen. There's too much at stake. My very sanity hangs in the balance. I phone my psychiatrist and tell him that I want to be referred to someone who's not as sarcastic as he is. From the prolonged silence that ensued I gather that no patient had ever dared to call him sarcastic or even ask to be referred elsewhere. I gave him the name of a psychiatrist whom a friend of mine had found helpful.

Years later, I was told that he had mellowed and had toned down the sarcasm. Does that take away the pain of those of us who suffered immensely under his dubious care? There is some damage that cannot be undone.

Where does the motto, "Do no harm" fit in? What is "harm" in his mind, in his estimation? What is harm? Do I hear an echo of Pilate's words? "What is truth?"

Eric Winthers

A long conviction of worthlessness
builds strong walls…
—Charles C. Finn

My therapist begins to emulate his mentor, my sarcastic psychiatrist, and sarcasm has now crept into our sessions. We are not making progress and my depression and confusion are being compounded by his aggressive attitude. He is frustrated, and so am I. Besides, I have not yet recovered from my last appointment with the afore-mentioned psychiatrist. I am still feeling emotionally overwhelmed, distraught and, as is usual, I am crying. And then my therapist bla-tantly lies to me.

The trust I had in him, that had taken so long to build up, is trampled. My mind reverts to childhood. Again, I become that hos-tile, abused child who had no one to trust, no one to believe in, no one to depend on. My anger, uncontrolled and childish, erupts. In a rage, I throw everything I can get my hands on—not at him—just everywhere. I do not want to hurt him. I just have to release the painful pressure of the emotions within me as they scream to get out.

There are words, so many words I want to hurl at him, words of truth, but they are prisoners within my tortured mind. These words come fast and furious, yet silently, in my head. In my head, I hear them. I yell them at him, mute.

"Don't lie. Don't lie to me! Aren't you here to help me? Yet you betray me with your lies. You tell me this process, this therapy, could have been shortened if I had gone into the hospital. Don't say it was my decision not to be hospitalized. No! No! Don't blame me. Remember—don't you remember? Both my husband and I agreed I should be in the hospital. We realized the severity of my depression. But you and my psychiatrist had a different agenda. You schemed, 'Diane is not depressed, and we can prove it. All it will take is time and sarcasm—unbounded sarcasm'."

I need to get away and to escape from my head. I get home and do what I know is the quickest way to escape from the pain, from the sobs that are threatening to choke me, and to escape from the voices that sound in my ears. I take some pills and down them with a drink. This will quiet all the voices. soon they will be gone, and tomorrow, maybe tomorrow, I won't feel the pain, the anger, and the hurt so much. Maybe tomorrow I will be better able to cope with the betrayal.

And then I am in emergency. The pills and booze have not yet worn off. The doctor asks "Did you and your therapist have a fight?" I do not answer. I protect him, my therapist. I am the parent now. That parent/child still lives within me. I take care of my brothers and sisters and others, like my therapist, I protect them. That is my job. I don't know any other way to be. I help them. Myself I cannot help. I do not protect myself; I have no worth. My worth comes from helping others. I am worthless. There is no *"me."* I have learned my childhood lessons well. How do you care for someone who does not exist?

The "blow up" was my fault. I'm guilty as usual. That's the way it always is.

Time passes. One day, I go back to apologize, but his office is empty. He no longer works there.

Dr. Christopher

Nothing in this world can take
the place of Persistence.

—Coolidge

And now I start over again. I am on the psychiatric ward of the University of Alberta hospital under the care of a gentle, compassionate, elderly psychiatrist. He has the task of picking up the pieces of the person that is me and preparing me for the outside world again. Very quickly, I am diagnosed as being clinically depressed. This had been vigorously denied by my previous psychiatrist which added greatly to my trauma and worsened my condition. I arrive here feeling as if I've been torn apart. I have frequent crying jags that speak of pain beyond words and I'm now even more fearful and guarded.

So the trial and error period of treating a chemical imbalance begins. Hopefully, finding an antidepressant that works won't take long. If the first one, or the first combination, doesn't work, we move on to another—and so the process goes.

The counseling starts, the talking starts, or rather my lack of it. Sadly, I am of little help. I dread each session, I answer the questions, but in spite of their kind, caring approach, I hide. I am a closed book and I do not want it read. I'm not ready. Maybe I'll never be ready. I'm so used to wearing my masks, to fooling the outside world, to putting up a good front that even this psychiatrist and his colleagues cannot break through the barriers. They cannot pinpoint the cause of my depression, even though they know that it must come from childhood. And I can't tell them. No, that's not true. I could tell them if I were brave enough, if I could overcome my own resistance.

It's my pride and my feelings of shame that keep me from telling them about my father's alcoholism and degrading treatment of his family and about how much I hated him and our life. I could tell him about my brothers' drinking and fighting and trips to the bootleggers and "cruising" for girls, and how ashamed and embarrassed I felt. I could tell them about the chaos, the yelling, the swearing, the foul language, and the crudeness that were part of my upbringing, the vulgarity of the life that shaped me.

Could I even mention the windows broken by thrown knives when my brothers fought, or my father slapping my mother when she refused to give him the "baby bonus" cheque which was usually used for our groceries and clothes, not his booze.

What do they know about a life like mine? How can I describe it to them? How can I describe the isolation, poverty, and hopelessness of my childhood, and what it felt like, to me, a sensitive, helpless child? How can I put into words the ugliness I lived? It was not words. It was always feelings: sad, lonely, poignant feelings. Those times when they ask about my father, how can I describe him to them? We lived in the same house, but I did not know him. He was my father, the enemy. If I talked about him, wouldn't my hate show through?

The child within me could tell them if she weren't so inhibited—so filled with shame and fear—fear of disclosing to them her "nothingness" and her shame-filled world. But she hurts too much and has no words, only tears and those she has already spoken. Tears that go back to a childhood, she cannot explain. Tears, she has shed enough for a lifetime.

I am that child again. I feel her emotions. Her tears are my tears, but I cannot describe the turmoil that rages within me. I have never had anyone to describe it to. I've never had anyone who cared. And what would they think of me if they knew all this? And how would I feel if I knew that they knew?

Shame is a powerful emotion. It can render a person mute and immobilized—part of the living dead. As I become familiar with my hospital surroundings and more aware of the other patients on the ward, another fear enters my consciousness. A frantic plea screams out silently within me, "Oh God, take care of my mind. Keep me sane." There are patients here that are so much sicker than I am. I question myself. "I'm not as sick as they are, am I? Or is it that I'm not their kind of sick? I'm not completely out of touch with reality, am I? Am I like some of them, the walking dead, a zombie?" My questions are many and go unanswered. "Oh Lord, keep me sane. I cannot take any more. I can barely cope with what's in front of me. In fact, I'm not really coping, am I? This is all beyond my capabilities."

I question God. "What is this life? What am I doing here? I do not understand. Oh God, take care of me. Is this your will? Why? Why me? Do I accept? Do I believe? What do I believe? Oh God, help me my unbelief." The words resound in the depths of my soul. They are my constant prayer when prayer is possible.

One of my therapists is not only a psychotherapist but also a part-time model. How can I relate to her or she relate to me? She is beautiful and talented. She is intelligent and educated. She is everything that I am not and never will be. In my mind she is perfect and I am a "nothingness." How can I open up to her. I can't. I don't. I'm not yet that courageous. Instead, I cringe and cry some more. This counseling seemed like an "exercise in futility".

Finally, I am given weekend passes to go home, but before Saturday and Sunday are over, I have crying jags for no apparent reason. I cannot cope. Even the familiarity of home is not what I need right now. My family has no idea how to help me and I can't help them. We are at a loss as to what to do. I'm terribly anxious, overly touchy, depressed. In short, a "bitch." I am glad and relieved when it comes time to return to the security of the hospital. I feel safe there. It has become my haven. This routine continues for quite a few weeks.

Depression is still very much alive in me. My mind wants to close in on me. I want to escape, to stay behind my wall of distrust and fear and depression. I want to disappear. I want to become invisible.

My psychiatrist and his team work to treat the chemical imbalance and the symptoms of my depression. But what I really needed was for someone to reach the wounded, hurting child within me to ease her fears and pain and to assure her that they were there to help and that life would be okay. But I am not yet receptive to counseling.

I was in the hospital for six weeks, four days, and eighteen hours. It felt like an eternity. As difficult as it was for me, it also took its toll on my family. By this time, my sons were in grade eleven and grade eight. There were many heart-wrenching moments that brought tears to my eyes then and that stay with me still. I had overwhelming feelings of guilt. This was my fault. No matter how hard I try, I can't do anything right. I am useless. I can't make it up to them. How do I go forward? How do I live?

Next came six years of follow up appointments. I held my own. I was feeling well enough but still had ups and downs. My medications were occasionally changed and counseling continued. There were many happy periods but they were always overshadowed by the bad. That was the way it had always been for as long as I could remember. It was as if I was still afraid of feeling good and enjoying it. When I felt good, I was anxious and fearful, just waiting, knowing that it would not last. It never did. I had learned that from a lifetime of sad experiences. Childhood had taught me well. Beware, even of happiness.

CHAPTER 29

Sunday Mass

In the Faces of Men and Women I See God.
—Whitman

I am at mass with my husband, and I am crying. I have been depressed, again, for a very long time and I "feel" no end in sight. I want to run away from it all—from everything, from everybody. But I can't. I am too tired. I don't have the energy to do anything. Life just isn't worth this struggle. Life makes no sense. In my mind, in my distorted thinking, the whole world is my enemy; even my husband has become my enemy. I want a divorce.

It is just after the consecration and we are holding hands with the couple who give the marriage preparation course. Even in my distraught state of mind this strikes me as ironic and I cry harder.

Others pray in unison, "Our Father who art in heaven" but my mind questions despairingly, "O God, if you were really here, would I even recognize you?" From somewhere comes the answer, "I am here." The words are as clear as they are unexpected. They stun my tears to silence. I drop my hands and look around and He is everywhere. He is everyone and everyone is He. Intuitively, without form, invisibly I see him present. This lasts one brief moment. For one brief moment, I felt I touched Divinity; or was it that Divinity touched me?

It was just one brief moment in time; one fleeting breath of eternity. In my heart, it will live forever.

Dr. Thomas

I have been in a city hospital for quite some time under the care of a very competent African American psychiatrist. Because this doctor has expertise in treating chemical imbalance, he was hand-picked for me by my last doctor before he retired.

In vain, my medications, which are many, have been juggled, but this depressive episode has proven to be especially resistant. So during my hospital stay I have undergone electroconvulsive treatments. These treatments haven't brought about any significant change. I continue to struggle with overwhelming feelings of sadness and guilt, of hopelessness. Fatigue and anxiety plague me. I most certainly don't feel ready to face the outside world yet, but my doctor is discharging me.

My reaction is violent, irrational, and instantaneous and shocking to him, his team of colleagues, and to my husband. I lash out in anger and racial slurs so hurtful and demeaning that afterwards, no one, not even my husband, will tell me what I said. I remember only my last words, "Let's get out of here."

I run back to my room and into the bathroom, where my nurse finds me sitting on the floor, sobbing hysterically. I have regressed to childhood. Once again, I am that angry, rejected child overwhelmed by the anguish of abandonment.

The whole world, even my doctor, has become my enemy. I cannot explain what is happening within my mind—the feelings that have engulfed me—that I cannot process. Depression is in control. This is all beyond my comprehension. I am merely a child and I go with what I feel, and I feel like I did as a child. I have no words, only tears. But they do not realize the fact that I am speaking!

How could my psychiatrist not see that I was now a child? With all of his education how could he not know what I later learned from a book? In *Homecoming* by John Bradshaw, Harvey Jackson explains the psychiatric term "spontaneous age regression." He writes, "The person in the grip of an old distress says things that are not pertinent, does things that don't work, fails to cope with the situation, and endures terrible feelings that have nothing to do with the present." No one had ever mentioned the word "flashbacks" to me. No one had ever told me that's what was happening when these episodes occurred.

My contact with the mental health system was now severed. My psychiatrist didn't want to see me again and he didn't refer me. If psychiatrists don't know what to do for me, who does? Hospitalization had been my desperate hope for recovery.

My husband and I drove home, but not in silence. I cried all the way. I had no words only more tears which I continued to copiously shed.

In the weeks that followed, my conscience gave me no peace. It nagged at me incessantly. *I was wrong*, it told me over and over again. I had insulted and embarrassed my doctor. And worse still, I had done so in front of his colleagues. Am I always wrong? Am I always the one who needs to ask forgiveness? Twice, I went back to his office in the city to apologize. The first time I was told abruptly, with evident hostility, that my appointment should not have been made. The next time, he made the gesture of accepting my apology and shook my hand perhaps just to get rid of me. Forgiveness was still in question, but for my part, I had done all I could.

It took a long time of confusion and more tears to recover from this episode—from this relationship. I am not sure if I ever really did.

CHAPTER 31

Marriage Counseling

And as this round
Is nowhere found
To flaw, or else to sever.
So let our love
As endless prove,
And pure as gold forever.
—Robert Herrick

My husband and I are starting marriage counseling for the second time. The first time, I had initiated the process, but this time, I left it up to him.

As usual, I'm nervous and I start the conversation with what I believe to be a simple truth. "It only took my husband a year to make this appointment." Immediately, without hesitation, without knowing me, without talking, without questions, I am judged by two seasoned therapist—the couple who are to counsel us. I have "attitude, a bad attitude." Consequently, "I have a problem. I am the problem." Their judgemental approach makes me cringe and I close down. I withdraw. I do not defend myself or try to explain. After all, they are the professionals. They are there to help me. Still, ingrained in me are those feelings of inferiority in the presence of authority.

I do not defend myself; I have not yet learned how. I still have no sense of self, of worth, of personal power. I am not yet a person, not yet real. There still is no *"me."* I listen only to others. I do not hear myself speak. I still do not recognize or understand all this that's happening inside of me. I cannot verbalize my pain, my thoughts, or my feelings.

My wounded child now hides within, beyond their reach. My tears are judged as unacceptable and are met with disdain and a tissue box is tossed across the floor to my feet. At this point I should walk out, but I don't; I am not strong enough. I still do not believe in myself enough, I leave the power with them. I dare not speak again and expose myself to more hurt and humiliation. How can I make them understand; I have no words, only tears, and no one is listening.

The self-talk of my depressive mind is speaking to me loudly with a barrage of mental distortions. "If they are right, then I must be wrong; I am always wrong. Why do I even try?" I cannot think or reason or make sense of this reality. "What is real, my mind or theirs? Am I completely out of touch?"

I have problems, pressing problems. How can I explain to these therapists, or to my husband that, when I am depressed, I sometimes perceive him as I did my father? I experience him as the "enemy." I hated my father. Do I hate my husband or do I hate what I feel he does to me, to us, especially when it's as painful as it is right now? I feel he has failed me. He has betrayed me. He has kept silent and his very silence has condemned me. The pain of betrayal is overwhelming. But I can't talk about this. It all seems too personal and even sinful. And even as my mind accuses him, I feel like I too, am a traitor. Do I love him? I cannot explain all that is playing out within my head. I cannot explain that when I am depressed my whole family seems to "change" and I can't relate to them. I can't connect with them. In my mind, they become "different" somehow and I can't talk to them and they can't reach me. At times I'm as cold and unyielding as a glacier. At other times I rage like a forest fire out of control. I still do not recognize the significance of all this; the depth of its meaning. I cannot express my fears and hurt—not here, not yet. It will be a long time coming. I still have so much to learn. But I do know that I must get this trauma outside of myself. I know that I must confront it. I must put these vicious feelings into words as judgemental and as sarcastic as they might sound. Still I'm unable to give them voice. My depression lies beyond words; my mind beyond reason. I struggle to hold it together. I don't want to try anymore. Living hurts too much. The childhood screaming starts inside of me again. "I can't, I can't. Just leave me alone, leave me alone. Jesus, Jesus, Jesus." Oh God, I am so weak, help me through this again and again and again. Help me to survive once more.

Our disruptive session finally ends and we return home and I cry some more. I cannot control the angry accusatory voices within my head. My self-talk rages. From the depths of my depression and tears, my thoughts continue to lash out at my husband mercilessly. "Why didn't you support me? How could you sit there beside me and let them crucify me? Why did you not defend me? You knew the truth—they didn't. They would have listened to you. They would have heard your voice. My voice was stifled the minute it sounded. I have no voice, only tears. But you're too accustomed to my tears. You've witnessed them all too often and still don't understand. Sadly neither do I, so I can't help you. I can't even help myself. If only you could hear my thoughts, would anything change, or would I lose you completely forever? I cannot take that chance."

"Do I fear getting better? Do I fear what it would do to you and me, to our family? What if I do change? Why is it I fear that someday I might wake up and not even know, not even like, this person I am married to—that I've been sleeping beside—that we have become strangers? What if feeling well means the end of us?"

During a subsequent appointment, it is decided that the woman will no longer counsel me but rather will mentor me. My husband doesn't need counseling, they've decided. My mind is working furiously, inaudibly it questions. "Is he perfect? The doctor who told me my husband is too good for me, was he right?" It is so hard to live with perfection when I am so flawed, so broken. Again, I am the guilty one. I am at fault. I am always guilty. The usual pleas of hopelessness start sounding in my head. "I can't, I can't, just leave me alone." Soon, my self-talk is drowned in my tears. I am lost, confused, and scared as I face the aftermath of marriage counseling.

And so I am being mentored by a therapist who claims she knows and understands where I am coming from. Yet she does not accept my depression. Instead she questions my need for, always, in her words, "putting on a face," referring to my lipstick and my habit of always having my hair "done." The connection between my need for counseling and my personal grooming eludes me. I do not question her observation. It sounds too accusatory and that I cannot deal with right now. Does my outward facade completely fool her? It must, if she does not recognize the signs of my depression that lie beneath my mask and sometimes, in fact quite often lately, break through.

During a severe depressive episode my marriage comes into question, always. Even a normal marriage has its ups and downs, however, these are magnified when one party suffers from depression. When a person is depressed, the problems are compounded; the anger and endless tears, the sarcasm and withdrawal and the lack of communication. Always, I have a foreboding feeling that it's too late, but too late for what? Too late for us? I have often felt that I was alone in marriage, so it is no surprise that I find myself alone in marriage counseling.

It hurts, unbearably. There are memories in my mind and in my heart that still hurt too much to write.

CHAPTER 32

Workshop for Depressed Women

I was enrolled in a workshop for depressed women and my assignment was to read the chapters on "Anger Management" and practice the principles until our next class. Over the week, I wrote these notes as I lived it.

I read all the material on "Anger" the first night. I had an immediate headache. I felt very upset, very emotional and stressed out, and very depressed. The next day, I felt sick, all over. I didn't volunteer at school. I did the essentials, made the meals and cleaned up; I washed a load of laundry and made a hair appointment for the following day but wasn't sure if I'd be able to keep it. I tried to work on my anger management, but I felt sick—body, mind, and spirit. I felt all the usual things that come when I'm angry and depressed—the headache, the tightness in the jaw, the neck and the shoulders, the heartburn and nausea and the feelings of hopelessness, of anxiety, and of sadness.

I was shocked and stunned at all the old feelings, the anger, and hate and depression that were stirred up and came surging to the surface. It was like living it all over again. Even the stuff I thought I had come to terms with kept going round and round in my head, and the old tapes of childhood kept playing. I knew I was turning inward and the wall was going up around me. I started shutting my husband out. I barely spoke; he had become the enemy again. Much of my anger was aimed at him, and as always, I was very hard on my sons. Then came the shakes, and everything in me began moaning, and groaning, and heaving, and sighing. Part of me just wanted to give up again, but part of me knew I could still rise above these feelings and try to quiet the "voices" and the turmoil within me. I had done it before. The next day, I forced myself to volunteer at the school, and when I got busy and distracted, it didn't hurt so much. I kept my hair appointment and shopped for groceries; and then I went for coffee with a friend. I was more in control, more reasonable.

Throughout the week I did very little housework and slept a lot—my usual escape. And every time I worked on the assignment I felt sick again. At one point, I resorted to tears of anger and helplessness. I felt more subdued, not so completely overwhelmed. I tried deep breathing, reading, and walking on the treadmill as I had been counseled. I phoned my sister and watched a couple of movies. Did that help? In a way, I guess, because I didn't lose myself completely during this time. I had what could have been a really "bad" week but it wasn't totally bad because I was able to maintain some control. Instead, it was just a very hard week. One in which I had to do a lot of positive self-talk to stay on track.

I had a very "conscious" week. I was very aware of what was happening, even the heartburn and migraine. I talked to myself a lot and I tried relaxation and meditation.

I went to a presentation called "Care for the Caregiver." It was a topic I was interested in since I was a lay counselor. Later that night, everything that had been covered kept going around and around in my head and I felt overwhelmed and inadequate thinking about, *how will I remember it all?* My rational response assured me, *I don't have to remember it all.* I have to trust that when I need it, it will be there, somewhere in my subconscious, and I can draw on it.

Next I had to face the weekend. My husband would be managing a hockey camp from Friday 'til Sunday night. That would mean he would be gone from six-thirty in the morning until almost midnight. This is his love, his passion. *I just wish I could find mine,* I thought as I faced the usual anger, criticism, and resentment. I kept telling myself, "Don't let the feelings take over. I know what I am thinking. I know what's bringing on these feelings? I can control them. I've done it before." If all of these events had gone negatively I would probably have withdrawn and reached the point where everything in me would have been screaming, "Leave me alone," and, "I can't, I can't." But that didn't happen. I held my own against the emotional demons within me and emerged stronger. This was a lot of work—hard work. It was rough.

Dealing with depression is hard because you can't see the negative forces that you're fighting. It's one thing to read or be told, "Strengthen your self-image. Keep a positive mental attitude or, you are what you think." It's another thing to work on these concepts daily and to feel like you're making progress. Personally I need something concrete, more structured to work with. "Anger Management" is a great start, but I feel that it focuses mostly on the symptoms and not the underlying causes. To continue working on the causes—the thoughts and feelings—the best tool I have found, so far, is Dr. Burns' book, *Feeling Good, The New Mood Therapy*. What I need now is a course on dealing with "Cognitive Distortions." Mine are still rampant.

Hell

During my seemingly endless recovery period, I attended a "Change ways Program" sponsored by Alberta Mental Health Services. This program, spanning many weeks, was designed to help people like me create positive changes in their lives.

Throughout the years I have taken advantage of every opportunity, in my search, to achieve wellness. I was still suffering major depressive episodes. It is a long process to heal one's mind, soul and life.

In the margin of my participant manual I wrote from my lifetime of experience:

Depression is Isolation and Isolation is Hell.
Hence Depression is Hell. I fear Hell.
I know Hell exists because I've been there.

Based on all of my searching, my in-depth probing and analysis, what have I learned that the professionals haven't? I have learned that there are some psychiatrists and researchers who claim that they don't really know where my type of depression comes from— chronic, endogenous, resistant depression. I find this rather disconcerting, frightening and, yes, depressing. I know exactly where my depression comes from. I maintain that I was born with it.

Like my stillborn brother, I too was stillborn, in so many ways, but I lived.

CHAPTER 34

"I Do Not Live; I Wait in Such Unhope."

I know what it's like to fight for my life. I have been deeply depressed for what feels like an eternity. My doctor has changed my medications once again, because the ones I was on have stopped working. It seems my body has become immune to them. I am going through that severely painful transition period. That period of trial and error which lasts until the new meds kick in. I plead, "Oh please, God, let them start working and soon." But there is no God in my world right now—or else he is not listening. If he were, wouldn't he make this go away, wouldn't he?

I know what it's like to barely exist, zonked out on new medications whose side effects are worse than the depression itself, if that is possible. I've lived that pain that rises from the depths of your being, that racks your body and traps your mind in its vice like grip. A pain that is mental, but also physical, cutting like a searing knife through my being.

Only a person who has suffered a severe depressive episode can relate to this, can understand, and can truly feel it. I'm told hospitalization is necessary. But I don't want the restrictions of a hospital setting. I need all the distractions that I can get. I need to see all the familiar things of home around me—anything that might ease the pain. Maybe, just maybe, they'll spark a memory of happier times. Maybe they'll give some relief.

I know what it's like to be an outsider, to have depression define me. I have suffered and I have lived depression in varying degrees of severity. I have lived that simmering hate and anger for everyone and everything—that depressive anger that can lie hidden, neatly draped, behind the curtain of a smile. I know what it's like to live behind a mask; to always hide my pain in public. I know that I must not let my facade drop and bring upon myself the stigma of mental illness.

When you say the word depression, I "feel" what you say. I even feel what you are not saying, what you cannot say, what you cannot find words to express. I have felt your pain, that pain that lies beyond description. I know where you're at. I've been there so often. I have lived there so long.

It was not one event, or two, or even a hundred that caused my depressions. It was my family's entire way of living and the feelings that went with it. It was the constant bickering, the strain of the confusion and unpredictability. It was the lonely lovelessness, poverty, and isolation—the hell. My young mind couldn't make sense of it because there was no sense. It was hopeless. Depression became familiar and familiarity felt good in my world of chaos. Like crying, depression was something I learned to do well. It became a part of me, and I was it. It defined me. I was conditioned from birth for lifelong depression. It came from around me; it came from within me; and it lodged itself deep within my psyche—depression which I battled for the rest of my life.

CHAPTER 35

Dr. Gifford

I idly chatter to you in the suave
tones of surface talk.
I tell you everything that's really nothing,
and nothing of what's everything,
of what's crying within me.
So when I'm going through my routine,
do not be fooled by what I'm saying.
Please listen carefully and try to
hear what I'm not saying,
what I'd like to be able to say,
what for survival I need to say,
but what I can't say.
—Charles C. Finn,
"Please Hear What I'm not Saying"

Over a period of eight years, I was in regular contact with a psychiatrist who considered me a "difficult case." But this seemed to appeal to him. It was a challenge not a threat nor an indication of my having a rebellious nature. *Was I that different from his other patients? And if so, how?* I wondered. I didn't feel free to ask. I still was not brave enough, so I wasn't told.

One time, he expressed a wish that he could be "a fly on the wall," just to see how I functioned in the outside world. It appeared that he, too, was anxious to learn. He gave me leeway and helped dispel some of the doctor/patient stereotypes of which I was so fearful. If my mind jumped from subject to subject, his followed. He did not completely control or impose his agenda on our sessions, and my questions were just questions and not efforts to undermine his authority.

I had always found it hard to think steadily on one subject for any length of time. To concentrate and to think constructively took a lot of effort. But I knew it was possible and I was anxious and willing to learn. These years were definitely a fruitful period in my ongoing learning process.

He once pointed out that I appeared to have signs of Parkinson's disease. I was stiff, robotic, with stifled, masked expressions. This could have been explained if I had been able and willing to describe my childhood to him—a time during which I felt I had to be prepared for any and every eventuality. I was constantly wary, uptight. In a world where there was no one to look after things for me. I needed to feel some kind of control in my hostile and unpredictable world. This kept me always on edge and always dealing with the "what-ifs" of my life.

At another session he told me I had all of the symptoms of having been sexually abused. I couldn't help him there. At the time I was working with him I had no recollection of having been molested, but his questioning must have triggered a recollection, because before long, I began having memories of childhood abuse. My therapist stepped in with "ongoing" counseling.

It was during this period of time that I worked extensively and in depth on the source of my feelings of sinfulness and shame; of inferiority and worthlessness; of being flawed, depressed and stupid. At my therapist's suggestion, I had a framed sign on my fridge which read "I love myself". A very basic and yet, in my case, a very necessary thing to do. How can you love others if you don't first love yourself? I remember, specifically, one of her confrontations. "If every time you asked God to help you to be the person he meant you to be, he did it. How would that change things?" Her question made me think and I believe it helped shift my mindset. I also realized that each time I had a setback, each time I was faced with a new and more challenging problem, I need not go back and start from scratch. I already had so much to build on. God, indeed, was busy shaping me. Unbeknownst to me, I was becoming the person he meant me to be.

I needed and sought the ongoing knowledge, skills, and perseverance to help establish a stronger, more active conviction. I needed to do this so that I could live a normal, happy, productive life. Still, at this stage, I needed constant non-traditional ways to boost my self-esteem and build self-confidence.

Throughout all of this my psychiatrist worked on the medical aspects of my depression using antidepressant therapy to deal with the chemical imbalance in my brain. There is no quick fix for depression. It's more like trial and error. And at times, that seems endless.

At one point, he changed my medications and warned my husband that I would probably become quite lucid. This lucidity didn't occur until a few years later. Everything happens in its own time, and my time was slow time. Or was it God's time?

During the course of treatment, Dr. Gifford completely debunked an earlier psychiatrist's opinion that I was not really depressed; that I was just acting. He assured me that, if I was not depressed, I was such an exceptional actress that I deserved an Academy Award. I would have settled for peace of mind.

He once wondered aloud what I would have become if I had a loving, nurturing upbringing. He saw in me a potential that had been stifled; potential that I had no chance to fulfill. For me, any idea of my potential was tempered by fear and the limitations my upbringing had imposed upon me. Fortunately, in time, I began to feel secure enough to let down some of my defenses—to lower the barricades behind which I had always hidden when I felt hurt or threatened or anxious or ashamed.

But even with this psychiatrist, my childhood secrets, for the most part, remained secret. Not even he came close enough to the real me to recognize and acknowledge the wounded, hurt child within. Not even he came close enough to say, "Hello, Diane, I know you're in there, and I'm here to help you to come out."

Yet I learned from him. I learned that I could hold my own in a mature setting. I began to realize, even more, just how great a part I had to play in my own recovery. I learned to believe more in myself as a person, I understood that I was depressed, but I was not stupid, as I so often feared.

If today I were to talk to this psychiatrist and therapist, I'm certain they would be proud but not surprised at the person I've become. I heartily thank them for their help in my recovery.

CHAPTER 36

Lecherous Old Man

…Forgive us our trespasses as we forgive
those who trespass against us…

One evening, I was visiting someone whom I rarely visited because the vibes I felt when I was anywhere near him were disturbing and demeaning. This particular evening, he was drinking as usual and hitting on someone else's wife. His actions triggered in me, an overwhelming sensory flashback—a spontaneous childhood regression. Like a piece of a puzzle falling into place, something clicked and my mind screamed in silent recognition. "You lecherous old man, you molested me when I was a child." What immediately surfaced were raw, gut-wrenching emotions.

The dirty, ugly feelings that were so much a part of my childhood engulf me, but now I knew where they came from. Once again, I feel the shame and sinfulness, the guilt and humiliation—all those loathsome feelings of disgust and degradation which I had kept buried deep inside for all those years. Those feelings had prevented me from being at ease in my own body, especially during adolescence. Those were the feelings that had been detrimental to my ability to accept my sexuality because I felt it was somehow dirty, defiled, and degrading. If someone made a crude joke, or a comment with sexual overtones, I would cringe with embarrassment.

Nothing could have prepared me for this evening's revelation; and nothing could have taught me how to respond, how to deal with it. These were recollections that I had relegated to the caverns of forgetfulness.

Perhaps it was shock that kept me silent as anger and disgust welled up inside of me. And, as is typical of my anger, I wanted to cry. But I didn't cry, not then, not there. The tears came later as I fought to accept this crudity of life.

The words of my psychiatrist came rushing back to me. "You have all the symptoms of having been sexually abused." But I had no recollection at that time, and I denied his diagnosis. Now, so strongly, I felt the pain of truth and betrayal.

There was nothing funny about this scene, and yet the words of a song rang through my mind. "Hold my beer while I kiss your girlfriend." It was all so absurd and disgusting.

Back into therapy I went—angry and shaken and tired but knowing full well that I had to deal with this, or I would never be free. Never again could I deny its existence to say, "That never happened to me."

He has changed, I hear. Perhaps age does that to a person. But some things cannot be changed—cannot be undone—even if a measure of forgiveness is reached.

My Mother-in-Law

From the time I left home until I got married, there was no one who got close enough to me to see me come completely undone in outbursts of depressive anger. My friends and neighbours may have seen some rough edges and experienced the impatience and irritability. But for the most part, in public, I was stoic and unyielding, which was sometimes mistaken for being "stuck up," when really what I felt was inferior. It took an enormous amount of energy to maintain the facade behind which I lived so as to appear to the outside world what I considered "normal." But at home, the mask could fall off and the facade could crumble as I went in and out of depressions—some lasting days, some weeks, and some even months.

It was always precarious when my mother-in-law would come to visit. While she was still working, she would come for two weeks during the summer and two weeks at Christmas. She lived too far away to make shorter visits. I could understand this.

An excerpt from my November 14, 1981, journal entry reveals my anxiety. "It's three weeks until my mother-in-law arrives. I'm not ready for her—mentally, emotionally, or even physically. I feel so drained right now. These past months have been so trying, so depressing. It's hard to imagine coping with the extra pressure I feel when she's around. I feel so tired and defenseless and hopeless. I don't really want to think about it any more than I want to think about Christmas and presents and cards and baking. All of these I like to get done before she arrives and hampers my efforts. It has been so difficult just doing the essentials lately. I feel I'm turning inward, wanting to hide, to escape, wanting to block life out, wanting to say, to hell with it all."

Sometimes it was not only her visits that precipitated a depression, but also the anticipation. It was a vicious circle.

Sure, she was family, but I had little concept of family connectedness. To me, she was part of that outside world and I believed that she must never see me depressed. For the most part, even if I was depressed, or if I had just come out of a depression, I could hold it together for her two-week visits. I prepared in my own distorted, shame-based way. In my ignorance and insecurity, I did what I presumed to be "normal." I'd clean the house from top to bottom. Isn't that what people did when company was coming? There must not be any reason for embarrassment or humiliation. I'd make sure there was no backlog of laundry or ironing so I could spend time with her. Every place I went, she went. This included coffee with my friends, shopping, trips to the beach, barbecues, supper out, and drives through the countryside. But most importantly my husband would take holidays so we could entertain her. We were living in northern Ontario at the time, so we made trips as far as Thunder Bay and James Bay just so she'd have something new to see, to experience. By the end of two weeks, I'd be getting tense and short-tempered, as depression would start breaking through and my resentment of the whole situation deepened.

When she retired, her visits lengthened to four weeks twice a year. That was too much for me. In that length of time, it was inevitable that I would suffer a depression. Just having "company" around every day for that length of time was too much stress, too much pressure. Impatience and hostility would build up, and by the end of her visit, I'd be in a deep depression which usually lasted for months. It seemed that I'd just get my feet under me and it was time for her next visit. The good times were hardly existent. As heartless as it might have been, we finally had to ask her to curtail her visits to two weeks. She only had one son and two grandchildren, so it was hard for her.

She never knew the real me as I was then, and if she had, I don't think she would have liked me. At least that's the way I felt. Maybe she would have understood and accepted my depressions; I don't know. We never spoke of it. I'm sure she had questions about me, but she never voiced them. She was too polite.

As she got older she suffered from osteoporosis which impacted everything she did. I felt as if I was going through old age with her, knowing that I would still have to experience this in my lifetime. I felt so apprehensive; at times it was overwhelming. It was hard to face the thought of suffering through old age twice.

Under normal circumstances, when I was feeling well, we got along fine and enjoyed each other's company. When my sons were born, they filled a lot of our time and life was easier. They were a shared interest—a bond between us. She was actually a lovely woman who had an air of elegance about her. She was congenial and had a genuine interest in our lives. She loved to help with the cooking and baking and I learned a lot from her.

She was not the problem. The problem was with me and my difficulty in having another person living in the house for that long. Even when I was first married it had been extremely difficult for me to get used to having a husband around. She had been a loving, caring, affectionate mother who raised her son alone from the time he was thirteen, when his father died. She was a great influence in his life, and he grew up to be independent and disciplined and loving—a remarkable man whom I was unbelievably blessed to marry.

CHAPTER 38

Dr. Joseph

Come Holy Spirit and Enlighten Me

It's another one of those downward spirals. I have been depressed for a very long time—that nagging, gnawing pain of chronic depression. Months have slipped by, and as often happens, neither pills nor prayers nor counseling have been able to break its hold on me.

Once again history repeats itself and I find myself on a hospital psych ward. Over a three-week period, I underwent a series of electroconvulsive treatments. Having patiently endured these, both my doctor and I know that they have brought about little change in terms of outward signs of improvement. And yet, as the days go by, I notice that something has happened within my mind. My old mindset has broken and some sort of enlightenment has occurred. I now know, without a doubt, that it is no longer my mind, but rather, my soul that is sick and hurting. I was on a psych ward but I knew with conviction that I no longer belonged there. There was no flashing light bulb moment. Instead, my epiphany came in a calm, quiet "aha" deep within my crying heart, my waiting soul. An "aha" meant for me alone.

I did not share my discovery, not even with my doctor. Perhaps I was afraid of how he'd accept this news. It was my diagnosis—a patient's diagnosis—so would he even believe me? Would he belittle me? Maybe I felt that he hadn't earned the right to hear it. In any case, it was my epiphany. After years of agonizing labor pains, it was I who had given birth to it. So significant was the change in my thinking that this point in my recovery became what I refer to as my second birthday. I had reached the point where I realized that I knew, and understood, more about myself than anyone—except God—ever would. And yet, at this point, I did not realize the true magnitude of what had happened, of what I had accomplished. This would take a few more years of searching and counseling, of prayer and self-reflection, and above all, the continuing painful process of becoming a real, true, free and authentic person. I felt there was little if anything left to talk about with this psychiatrist—at least anything that I was willing to divulge. During my days in the hospital we had not made a meaningful connection. He never reached the wounded and depressed child within me.

As I was being discharged, Dr. Joseph gave me what he called his "humble opinion." He suggested that my depression was "habit." As he said the word "humble" to qualify his diagnosis, the word "pompous" crossed my mind. But I needed more than a questionable diagnosis. If my depression was merely "habit," it was a habit that I must have developed very early in my childhood to help me survive. It was a habit that I must have adopted in order to deal with the world—that hostile world that otherwise might have engulfed me—a vulnerable, helpless child. For me, this habit was normal. It was my habitual way of living. It was me. But if it was all that simple, why have I been in the mental health system off and on for more than forty years? Why have all these psychiatrists been treating me for all these years? I didn't bother asking. At this point, it really didn't seem to matter. It wouldn't have changed anything. I was just glad to get out of there.

My psychiatrist offered little professional help, suggestions, or support as to how to deal with his "diagnosis." My doctor failed me.

No, he didn't fail me, he failed himself. He failed to make any connection between what I had been and what I had become.

This was my last trip to any psych ward. Perhaps I had my fill of psychiatrists—humble ones, pompous ones, sarcastic ones, even caring, compassionate ones. Maybe I felt that I was well enough to try it on my own. Very slowly, I had been learning how to live.

PART

3

Anecdotes of Darkness

CHAPTER 39

Christmas

Out of the depths I cry unto Thee...
—Psalm 130:2

It is just after Christmas. I am driving up the highway towards home, crying uncontrollably. Everything in me is screaming, "There is no God, there is no God." Tears blur my vision as they keep rising up from the depths of me. I have just had another disastrous session with my therapist, and I've been pushed over the edge of depression into that deep dark pit of despair.

My world has turned dark and ugly. The enemy is all around and inside of me. It's screaming, "There is no God, there is no God." I have to get away from my head; it's going to explode. The pain is too intense, I cannot bear it. I have to escape, if only for a little while. The need is overwhelming. I have lost all hope, all control. I get home and I take the crucifix off the wall and smash it against the end table into so many pieces. "There is no God, there is no God." Where, oh where, is my faith? It's not here, not now. I take some pills and a drink and I lie down to wait for oblivion to wash over me.

But then the Christmas tree speaks to me. It says, "If there is no God, what am I doing here?" I get up. I grab a Christmas gift, one of my son's ski poles, and I thrash the Christmas tree. "There is no God, there is no God." In my mind, in those moments of despair, there is no God. I am Peter, I am Judas. I deny and I betray. I am a sinner; I am guilty. I am always guilty.

My husband and son return home and clean up in silence.

When I awaken from my drug-induced respite, my pain's intensity has lessened. My storm has abated. My family doesn't ask the question that must plague them—questions they know that I can't answer. They know that they have witnessed another of my dark nights of the spirit. They have witnessed many. So many sad, disturbing memories for my family to bear.

CHAPTER 40

The Ticket

I am driving through a school zone, but this does not register with me. My mind is in turmoil and I am crying. I have just had another devastating session with my therapist; he has beaten me down completely and left me feeling lost and hopelessly overwhelmed.

I have always found counseling sessions traumatic. I learned as a child not only to hide my problems but also myself. I'm still too ashamed and guarded to talk about myself, my family or our lifestyle, or to reveal the real me hidden behind my many masks. My therapist might be feeling frustrated again, but how does he think I feel? I lived it all and am still living it. Right now, this is the best I can do.

The police officer pulls me over and issues me a ticket for speeding. As he hands it to me, he says, "I hope the rest of your day goes better than it has so far." I keep crying. That is the most empathy, the most compassion that I have been offered this day.

Sometimes counseling falls so short of its goal, of what it is actually meant to accomplish.

Out with "Friends"

I am in a restaurant for supper with two of my friends. They talk to each other quite exclusively. As dinner progresses the old childhood feelings of being a non-person, start welling up inside me. It becomes disturbing. I do not want to go back to that pain. I wonder, "If I went to the restroom and didn't come back, would they even notice?" I am tempted, but I do not leave. I think to myself, "Had I been invited, or did I invite myself?" I do not ask because, as in childhood, I would rather be hurt than to hurt another. Right now I am hurting.

Those feelings of being an invisible person still lay within me and at times like this, they are awakened. Once again, I feel like a "nothingness." In psychiatric terms, I go through a "spontaneous age regression" and become a child again. Unfortunately, I haven't yet learned about this concept and so I withdraw. I hide in silence.

CHAPTER 42

Suppertime

For better or for worse, in sickness and
in health, 'til death do us part.

I have said that, for most of my life, living has been synonymous with depression. To further complicate life, my depressions have been synonymous with anger.

I am in the kitchen preparing supper. It is a suppertime like no other suppertime. I have a butcher knife in my hand and I'm confronting someone face-to-face and I'm screaming in a frenzied fit of depressive anger. The reason, it does not matter.

I have felt that uncontrolled rage that leads to violence, to assault with a deadly weapon.

I have been to that point where a person acts in ways completely foreign to them. That deadly urge—it's mine, but yet beyond me.

I have felt that overwhelmingly evil desire to strike, to stab, and to kill. You don't have to plan; you don't even have to think. Surely Satan takes over.

Yes, I have felt those last precious moments just before you become a murderer.

A compelling voice cuts through my insanity and orders me, "*Don't Do It.*" The danger passes, and sanity returns. I remember, so well. I remember. It jars my heart. It makes me shudder.

In an instant of unbridled passion, I almost changed the course of our lives—the lives of my whole family—forever.

As accustomed as he was to my tirades, I don't know if my husband knew. I don't know if he realized the seriousness, the danger, of those last few moments suspended in time. I've never been brave enough to ask. Some words are best left unspoken. Some questions are best left unanswered. Perhaps some truths are not meant to be shared.

Looking back confirms my belief in miracles. There have been many miracles in my life. I thank God for each and every one of them. I especially thank Him for His forgiving and merciful love.

Walk-in Clinic

Man's inhumanity to man makes
countless thousands mourn.
—Robert Burns

I am in a city hospital undergoing a medical procedure for which I have been given Demerol. At this particular time, I am going through a major depression and I don't know where to turn. The doctor, realizing that my depression and my physical ailments are related, refers me to a certain walk-in clinic. I go there by taxi.

Still woozy from the painkiller, I go through their humiliating intake process with tears and truthfulness. Perhaps too much truthfulness! My answers to their questions are met with a measure of amusement and certain disbelief. They hear what they want to hear and their insinuations come through loud and clear. I've just had Demerol? You must have good connections to get Demerol! I drink Kahlua in my coffee? Winos can't afford Kahlua! I meet an endless barrage of sarcasm. I am treated like a "junkie" and a "wino." I feel judged and ridiculed. I feel degraded—a little less than human.

My mind is in pain and chaos. I cannot think. With much difficulty and more tears I struggle through the written questionnaire.

I am very slow, so it is not possible, in my present condition, to list my nine siblings and their birthdates or to answer pages of similar questions regarding family relationships. I cannot explain or defend myself. Besides, I have no words, only tears. And they don't want tears or explanations. I am told sarcastically "It doesn't have to be perfect."

It is closing time. I ask to use their telephone to call a taxi, and I am told, "There's a pay phone down the stairs."

In a corner of the stairwell, a man is crouched in abject despair. I feel his pain, his desperation, and I cry harder. But now I am crying, not just for myself, but for him, and for all the people like him, who don't have the support of a family like mine or the wherewithal to keep fighting for help in a health care system that is failing us.

There are times when this encounter still comes back to haunt me, and I cry. This is worthy of everyone's tears.

CHAPTER 44

My Husband Says

> …Please listen carefully and try to
> hear what I'm not saying…
> —Charles C. Finn

It's the usual question, "What is the matter with Diane?" My doctor and nurse walk into my hospital room and he asks quite matter-of-factly. "What's going on? Your husband says you've been feeling quite good." I could tell them what's going on if only I could find the words to describe the indescribable what, so far in my life, I've been unable and unwilling to describe, the hell that is within me. I could tell them what's going on. It's very simple. I just don't want to live. I long to die. But if I tell them that, then they would think I'm crazy, wouldn't they? I know I'm not crazy. But life has, once again, become too much of a struggle; too painful. It's not worth it. If I could find words for these distorted thoughts and feelings I could tell them. I could tell them, but the words are welled up inside of me, and lost in tears. Why doesn't anyone understand that my tears are my words, they speak volumes. These people do not understand this language that I'm speaking.

Instead, the doctor's words have sent my depressive mind reeling out of control in anger and disbelief. "My husband says, my husband says" rings loudly in my ears, and my mind questions. "Why do they listen to him and not to me? Does he feel my feelings, my pain, this pain that is all encompassing and oh so isolating? Is he in the darkness of despair that I'm lost in right now? Does he speak for me? Do I not have a voice yet? Are my thoughts and feelings not valid? Will my judgement, my opinions, ever have worth? Will I ever be heard? These words dammed up within me. Will they ever be vocalized? Am I not a person yet?"

My distorted thoughts come fast and furious—tangled, and jumbled. Intense feelings have been evoked that I still cannot understand or explain or control. I am lost once again, trapped in the world of childhood emotions and silence. I do not recognize; I cannot reason; I cannot name the feelings that assail me. I have descended to the depths once again. I cannot cope.

It is years before I figure out that it all goes back to that child of long ago who was never a child; who was never heard; was never validated; but who is now struggling to emerge. I do not understand the desperate struggle for personhood that rages within me.

They are startled and perplexed when I cry out to them rudely, bluntly. "Just leave me alone. Leave me alone." My doctor and nurse leave me. As they depart, the child within me cries out in silent words. "No, no, that's not what I mean, that's not what I need. It's not what I want. Please don't leave me alone. Don't abandon me. I've been alone all my life. It's not you that I want to leave. It's this darkness and despair. It's this depression that I want gone from my life. I need you I cannot do this alone. I have tried for so long." But the words don't come. I cannot yet verbalize it. I cannot reach them with my soundless words.

Again I have regressed to childhood and I act as I did as a child. They cannot reach me. I am lost and alone and hurting beyond description. I need someone to rescue me. I hide from their words, "Your husband says," like a child does when reprimanded unjustly with no explanation. Will anyone ever hear me? Will anyone ever understand me? The "leave-me-alone tapes" are playing loudly in my head. I can't process any of this. Unwittingly, I am my own worst enemy. At this stage, the greatest impediments to my being understood, and to recovery, are my silence and tears, my resistance to disclosure. But I have no words yet. I am a child and all of this is beyond my comprehension. I am still without speech.

I question God. "Why do they leave me alone? Why do they abandon me? Can't they feel my pain? Can't they just sit with me and let me cry, to speak my words in tears, the language of my childhood. Oh God, help me through this again; deliver me. I want to be made whole, a normal person. Oh God, be with me. Help me to survive."

In my own terminology, I have "crashed." I have lost myself in my depression. I cry and I sleep. I sleep and I cry day in and day out. I am so very tired. Just let me cry and sleep. This process has taken place so many times before. But I need time. I need time to recoup. Although I do not know it yet, time is my friend. It is giving me much needed insight, ever so slowly.

PART

4

Rebirth

New Ideas, New Challenges

During all those years, I continued to believe that the answers to all my problems lay in knowledge. I was obsessed with finding a name for what was wrong with me. I thought that if I could figure it out, then it could be treated. With this in mind, I started reading every self-help and psychology book I could get my hands on. I searched relentlessly. When my husband's work required him to go into the city I would sometimes go with him. I'd browse through bookstores for hours, searching for something that sounded familiar; something that identified the symptoms I was experiencing. Gradually, I built up quite a library of two hundred or more books. Some books I read in their entirety and even reread; some, I perused or read parts of; a few I discarded as irrelevant; and a couple became my second bible.

As a youth, and now as an adult, I was very idealistic. I lived on "feel good" mottos and quotations, even unrealistic ones, as they pertained to me. I discovered the Psycho-Cybernetics series by Maxwell Maltz, MD, and set out to change my mind set. Did they help? They were a very good start and above all they kept my hopes alive and gave me goals to aim for. Even on my way to work I'd recite the poem I had taped to the dashboard in the car—"This is the beginning of a new day…"

I was introduced to Dr. Burns' *Feeling Good: The New Mood Therapy*. I successfully struggled through a couple of workshops based on the book and began confronting my many "cognitive distortions." One of my biggest problems was that I wanted complete answers. I wanted to reach a point of certainty—of complete wellness. I had not yet accepted that it doesn't exist. Recovery is an ongoing process; it is a painful and time consuming undertaking. So I often wanted to give up. It hurt so much. My fight for a healthy balance, which so many take for granted, was a challenge akin to an obsession, for which I am now thankful because my life depended upon it.

This stage of my life spanned three decades; three decades of work, of countless depressions, and doctors appointments, of hospitalizations and psychiatrists, of medications and counseling, and endless tears. It took all those years for my life to start coming together, to start making some sense.

Gradually, during those years, something happened with, or in, my thinking process. What would have bothered me, what would not have been adequate, or perfect enough, became acceptable, even by my critical standards. I was no longer ashamed of myself, my looks, my actions, or even my thoughts and intentions, or my way of living. Little by little, my depressive episodes lessened in frequency, intensity, and duration. I became more spontaneous and more productive and could sense a purpose to my life—a feeling that I had something to contribute.

That is not to say life became easy. It just became more normalized. I could accomplish more with less effort. I related differently to my family. I was more in control but not completely aware of what I had accomplished—and far from satisfied.

I had learned to easily say, *"I," "me,"* and *"my."* I had to take responsibility for my thoughts, for my opinions, for my life. I no longer feared being wrong or needed to be perfect. I accepted myself as human. Normal, for me, was no longer that wounded child who was raised in shame and sadness. I rose above that hopelessness and now could say, "That was me then; this is me now." I learned to accept myself with all of my weaknesses and weirdness, but also with all of my gifts and virtues. I achieved an acceptable measure of selfhood and I could see myself for what I am—a loved and loving child of God.

I suffer from depression, but depression is not my identity. I am more than that. I am a wife, a mother, and a grandmother. I am a sister, a friend, a volunteer—a person just like you striving to do my best and hoping to make a difference in this world. I am *"me,"* and there's seldom a day goes by that I don't thank God for my life; the life I so often wanted to throw away, the life I so often wished away.

My recovery from depression has given me a greater understanding of how my mind works and a greater self-awareness. My spirituality has deepened and I have grown immensely in compassion and resiliency. Yet, even today, to maintain my mental health, I need constant reminders to live in the "now," to practice "mindfulness." That helps take away the pain of the past and fear of the future.

I still have my ups and downs, but nothing compared to my childish, explosive outbursts of the past. The child within me has found a certain peace.

I do not know when all the strands of my life began to weave together to form a patterned whole. But I do know that I took the final steps in my search to fill that God-shaped space within my heart when I started going to daily mass.

I had often read about the proverbial light at the end of the tunnel. What I discovered was that the tunnel lay within me. So the light also had to come from within me. In time it did.

CHAPTER 46

Rounding the Corner

For the next few years I struggled with the dilemma of trying to figure things out on my own. Then, as fate would have it, I came across two books that helped me greatly. The first was *Homecoming: Reclaiming and Championing Your Inner Child*, by John Bradshaw. The second, by Charles L. Whitfield, was *Healing the Child Within: Discovery and Recovery for Adult Children of Dysfunctional Families*. They were, for me, a font of information. They shed light and understanding on my lifelong struggles. They were truly a godsend.

The information I gleaned inspired me. In light of what I read, I moved on to examine and better understand where my childhood traumas originated. I arrived at the source of my distorted views of life: my negative, depressive way of thinking, and my endless feelings of guilt and shame, of lonely hopelessness and of despair, of worthlessness.

Above all I came to understand what I had been exhibiting off and on all my life—spontaneous age regressions. When I was raging and lashing out at my family in uncontrolled fits of anger, I was actually reliving parts of my childhood. Some event or occasion, words, or even someone's attitude could trigger this regression and transport me to the time of the original hurt when depression was my defense against the pain—the hell—of childhood. Depression was a reprieve. It was a place I could go to hide when I could not express what I felt due to a lack of words, fear of the repercussions, or punishment.

I was now able to seriously start working on healing these wounds from the past. The most cathartic was writing and listening to the stories of my siblings about how they had survived living under the same roof as I did, yet so little I really knew about them. We had never experienced that healing power of storytelling as we grew up. We had been of little help to each other.

What spurred me on was knowing that I was on the right track. I realized that so much of what I had been fighting for all my adult life, so much of what I had been doing was right. It was what I had to do. I had been re-educating myself. But with over half-a-century of my life behind me, I could now understand why this had been proving to be such a formidable task. To educate is one job, but to re-educate, meant I had a lot to "unlearn," to discard. I also had to accept that there was so much that a normal, happy child would have learned during their formative years that I might never learn. I just wouldn't have enough time.

I had made a new beginning. I had opened up to the person that mattered the most: me, myself. My focus shifted. It is very difficult, almost impossible, to describe this phenomenon. Like the final pieces of a puzzle falling into place the picture of my life had changed. It was as if, for all these years, I had been looking at a certain picture not realizing that it was hanging upside down. But gradually, imperceptibly, it had shifted; it had turned until now I finally saw it, as it was meant to be viewed. This was definitely a momentous eureka moment. This truly was my second birthday. I was reborn.

However something was still missing. I couldn't put a name to it but I felt it in the very depths of me. It presented as a haunting call for purpose which emanated from a hole within my soul. Somewhere within me, a new paradigm was evolving; a sane, more normal, balanced life was developing for me. I began searching for that which would nourish my soul. Unfortunately it can be as challenging to find good help for the soul as it is for the mind or the body. In spite of the drawbacks of depression, or maybe because of them, my spiritual journey, rooted in my Catholic faith had begun in childhood. I never lost that gift from God.

As much as I knew, and in spite of all of my years of learning and experience, I had no idea how or when all the scattered bits and pieces of my life would come together. In fact, at this point, as usual, I didn't realize that they had to come together before I would feel completely well, completely whole, alive and spontaneous, creative and loving, fulfilled.

Would I, and patients like me, have been spared years of suffering if, at some point, this method of treatment—healing-the-inner-child workshop—had been used? Obviously, knowledge of this approach was out there, available, I found it, albeit quite accidentally. On my own initiative, I was able to use it and to assimilate it with noticeable success.

Could I, and patients like me, have benefited more from this approach than from a series of psychiatrists. Or was this the way my life story was destined to play out?

EMDR – Eye Movement Desensitization and Reprocessing

When our local Lay Counseling Organization was formed, I was one of twelve people to take the course. I felt that, after all I had suffered and survived, I had something to give to others. We started doing volunteer counseling in such areas as self-esteem, depression, sibling rivalry, and marriage counseling. We dealt with clients whose problems were less serious than those of people waiting to get into the over-crowded, public mental health system.

I was still going through depressive episodes myself, but not as often, and they were not as severe or as long lasting.

It was during lay counseling training that I started considering EMDR (Eye Movement Desensitization and Reprocessing). I had read about EMDR and questioned whether it was a method of treatment I should try. The technique is associated mostly with post-traumatic stress disorder (PTSD) victims like "shell-shocked" soldiers returning from war. I had been at war all my life. It was an internal war, a war that raged inside of me and kept me prisoner within my own mind, a war inflicted on me by the abuses of childhood and my family's constant chaotic, and unpredictable lifestyle. As well as I was feeling, nothing had erased the residual pain of these childhood traumas. Counseling had helped somewhat, but I felt the need to focus my attention elsewhere for more in-depth healing.

PTSD is characterized by intrusive thoughts and memories which can cause serious anxiety disorders, issues of self-esteem, depression, nightmares and, as in my case, vivid flashbacks. When I spoke to my psychiatrist about EMDR, I was told that I needed specific events from my past to work with. I couldn't work with forty years or a lifetime of events in general. The word "specific" clicked with me. A lifetime of "specifics" lay buried within my heart. I went home and wrote about twenty occasions in my past that had traumatized me. They weren't nearly as serious or devastating as what other people might reveal, but to me, they were important. Their importance had not registered with me before.

Armed with my list of "specifics," I consulted with an EMDR therapist. The therapist used the EMDR method at intervals to target and reprocess my ugly, unwanted memories stemming from the specific events I had identified.

No one completely understands how EMDR can take traumatic thoughts and memories and allow them to be reprocessed by the mind which allows them to change or fade in their intensity. EMDR mimics rapid eye movement (REM) sleep and it is believed that during REM sleep, the brain finds ways to unlock and heal trauma that had previously been locked into the nervous system. Just as the body knows how to heal wounds, so too the mind has the ability to heal itself. We are not prisoners of memories.

In the throes of one of my crying jags, my therapist told me that I was more in touch with my emotions than with my spirituality. I did not refute her. She was the professional. It was, after all, just one more blow to add to my emotional stockpile. Later, I questioned her need, or right, to judge my spirituality. Even I leave that to God. I was quizzed about my beliefs and experiences and relationship with God and I, very compliant, tried to answer as best and as honestly as I could. This was not of my own choosing. Then there were the more mundane questions: Did I want to get a tattoo? Did I like my name or would I like to change it? To do such things was supposed to be helpful in finding my true self, in establishing my own identity. Such things, to me, were out of the question. And even if I had thought about them, they wouldn't have appealed to me.

I was asked to describe my favourite place to go to relax—Jasper Park Lodge was my response. I described the lake scene as truthfully as I could. I was told that it sounded like a weather report. I still was not free enough to trust my own perceptions—the sights, the sounds, the touch of the wind that I experienced. I still could not claim what was mine. I was not accustomed to using words like "I, me, and mine."

It was later, after I finished the EMDR sessions, that I came up with the idea of putting the first letter of my second name, Brenda, before my signature to proclaim that I should be B. Diane Summers—B. "Me."

At first, I didn't think EMDR had made a difference. But gradually, I came to realize that something had happened; something had changed. The past didn't seem to matter as much anymore. It was losing its grip on me. I could finally think of my childhood without crying. A certain amount of resolution had been reached.

But there was still an emptiness within. I had not yet found what my soul was searching for.

Father Eugene

When the Pupil Is Ready, the Teacher Will Appear.

One day I was talking to someone, expounding upon my many unresolved problems and feelings. Like any other good therapist he listened patiently and said very little.

As I talked I touched on situations that shame had caused me to keep hidden and problems that seemed insurmountable—current ones, and especially ones reaching back to childhood. I delved into feelings I had felt I could never let go of, and relationships, and of people to forgive who seemed to me unforgivable. Many such feelings still hurt my heart and brought tears to my eyes. As I was leaving, he quietly mentioned, "Mass is at five o'clock." Just five little words, that turned my life around. I live six houses away from St. Joseph School Chapel, but the idea of attending daily mass had never occurred to me. There's an old saying, "When the pupil is ready, the teacher will appear." And I was finally ready.

I have been at five o'clock mass almost every day since. That I am able to do so is, in itself, a blessing. The mass nourishes me and gives purpose to my day. It is mending my "brokenness." But the mass is not something rather it is SOMEONE, and that person is

Christ. It is Christ who is healing the sickness of my soul and filling that depthless void within me. It is Christ, the Eucharist, who speaks to my heart. It is He who is the true answer to the life that I was searching for. I found my source and my center in God, in love, and I've never looked back.

Zen Buddhists have a *konan* (a riddle) that asks, "What was your face before your parents gave birth to you?" Thomas Merton asked a similar question, "What is my identity?" I think his response answers both questions.

> "To say I am made in the image of God is to
> say that love is the reason for my existence,
> for God is love. Love is my true identity. Love
> is my true character. Love is my name."

Years later, I learned that spirituality is the final stage in recovery. Spirituality is about the relationship that we have with our self, with others, with the universe, and with God. It is not knowable merely through our intellect or through reason. It must be lived. It is that ongoing process that reaches through suffering and healing to serenity and peace.

Dr. Francis

There is a saying from the Talmud that "Whoever saves one life, it is as if he [or she] has saved the whole world."

I am especially grateful that, in my fight for sanity and selfhood, I was blessed with one doctor, Dr. Francis, who had the patience and took the time, so much time, to listen not only with his head, but also with his heart. He knew what it meant to be a doctor and he treated me, the person, and not just my symptoms.

In the beginning, he sat with me through countless tearful appointments. Not knowing if I would ever stop, he would just tilt his stool back precariously and let me cry and cry. He accepted me just the way I was, completely broken and, in my own eyes, a "nothingness." He seemed to understand that this was a stage I had to go through, a period of grieving, before real healing could begin. Beyond the adult/child who cried before him, somehow he saw the person I was meant to be, and by his quiet, non-judgmental presence, he validated that person who hid deep inside of me and was struggling to come out, to be born. This grieving was essentially the beginning of my lengthy recovery process. Someone other than me believed my pain, accepted my depression, and was willing to help me confront it and learn to deal with it. The groundwork which he and I established was crucial. I built my selfhood on it.

He once told me to "live my life," but I was not ready for such a concept. It still lay beyond my comprehension. I had always lived through others and for others. There was no *"me."* No "my life." I could not live what I did not know.

I would cry an ocean of tears before I learned to trust enough to risk speaking. It wasn't much at first, but it was a beginning. However, even to him I still did not disclose the source of all my anguish, that personal hell that burned within me. Its roots were mine to find and come to terms with. Those roots, I found, were steeped in toxic shame that had kept me mute and immobilized since childhood.

In the security he provided, I began to examine my warped perceptions of myself and of all life. Ever so slowly, I managed to break down some of my protective walls, to shed some masks, and begin the ongoing process of becoming real—a person in my own right. Unraveling my childhood was most painful and revealing. The revelations I unearthed and put to rest were a vital part of my recovery.

Mental illness had been a lifelong part of me and was deeply rooted in my psyche. My recovery spanned so many years and was so gradual it seemed almost imperceptible. As psychiatrists, therapists, counselors, and general practitioners came and went through the years, Dr. Francis remained, the normalizing, dependable force I so desperately needed and relied on. He was not a god, but to me, he was akin to a saviour. He was my hope. During those times when I felt life was not worth living, when I wished I was dead, hope alone kept me alive.

His sudden death was devastating. And it woke in me an emotion I had never truly experienced before. For the first time in my life, I felt real sorrow. You know the kind that breaks your heart and tells you that life will never be the same again.

I regret that he never got to meet the real me that emerged from my anguish and tears. At the time of his death, I didn't yet realize the magnitude of the miracle that had been wrought within me. I was well on my way to recovery.

Two year later, I began to write; to put into words my journey through depression. I had so much to say, but who do I say it to? To everyone.

His spirit lives on as I live; and I live in wellness. He was my doctor, my mentor, my friend, and I loved him dearly. I owe him a debt of gratitude that lies beyond repayment.

When I was a child, crying was the only thing that felt good. Now sometimes, as if I know a secret, I feel like I am smiling deep inside within my heart.

Only a heart
can utter gratitude
to another heart

So my heart speaks. "Thank you, Dr. Francis. This is my tribute to you. I pray you rest in peace, and I hold you in my heart."

CHAPTER 50

Home Again

They say that, as an adult, you can never go back home again. Once I left home at the age of sixteen, I never had any desire to go back. There was nothing there for me except sad and bitter memories, and tearful reminders of the isolation and loneliness I had lived with and struggled so hard to cope with. I didn't want to ever dredge up those feelings of shame and degradation if I could possibly avoid it. I felt none of the normal nostalgic attachments to family and home; none of the normal feelings of belonging, of kinship, of love. I had no desire to belong to this family I lived with. Even as a child, I wanted to get as far away as I could, if only I had known some place to go. If only I had not been so fearful of the world out there, if only, if only.

I was in my forties before I could even think about my childhood without crying. Any fleeting happiness I had experienced was always overshadowed by the depressive pain. The angry, neglected child still lived within me. The feelings were still so intense, so ingrained in me. The few times that I went back, it was more because of a sense of duty than of love. Love was not part of my childhood.

Many years later, as a happily married mother of two grown sons, I was well on my way to recovery. Together with some of my siblings, I returned to search for that first house of my childhood. It could not be found. It didn't have a cement foundation and had succumbed to the ravages of time. It was as if it had never existed—that unpainted square house that, during my earliest, formative years, had shaped me in shades of black and grey with memories that were even darker.

Yes, it had virtually disappeared and I found that the feelings that had been given birth there had lost their intensity. They no longer had their demonic hold over me.

Going home without my sorrow
Going home sometime tomorrow
Going home to where it's better
than before
Going home without my burden
Going home behind the curtain
Going home without this costume
that I wore
—Leonard Cohen

God and My Depression

In my later years, it was pointed out to me that we all have our crosses to bear. I had heard this saying many times before and I believed it. But this particular time caused me to consider it differently. If depression was my cross to bear, then it was God's will for me. If it was God's will for me, I should not only accept it, but I should embrace it.

Depression took on a whole new dimension. My job was to align my will with the will of God. St. Teresa of Calcutta says, "Suffering is not a punishment, not a fruit of sin, it is a gift of God. He allows us to share in His suffering and to make up for the sins of the world." Depression still remains a disease that I have to cope with. But I finally "got it." It now has new meaning in my life. It has become my suffering offered up as a loving self-sacrifice.

If I had my way, I would still prefer to have my sufferings all wrapped up in neat manageable packages. That way I could open them one at a time, a little at a time, when I feel brave enough to deal with them when my trust in God, who will "never give me more than I can handle," is strong enough.

CHAPTER 52

My Sons

I have been blessed with two sons who, in spite of my many depressive upheavals, grew up to be loving, remarkable young men. With all my heart, I regret the pain and suffering I put them and their father through. I thank them from the bottom of my heart, without end, for bearing with me, especially when we saw no end in sight. To my sons, I say, "I love you dearly, I have from the day you were born and even before that. During your years spent at home, I would have shown you more love and respect if only I had been able. If only I had reached maturity before motherhood. If only I had not been an adult-child. And, perhaps then, I would have not missed so much of your childhood."

I have memories of my sons that warm my heart and make me smile. Paul was the studious one, the one I found at two-and-a-half years old sitting on the vacuum cleaner, in the broom closet, "reading a book." He later became our navigator on holidays. He had the travel books and the information, mostly in his head. He kept us up to speed on what we had seen and what lay ahead that we were about to see. Paul was more inquisitive, the archeologist type. His rock collection was kept by us when he left home. He still hasn't reclaimed it. We missed him a lot when he graduated from high school and moved on to university. His quiet presence had filled a great need in our home and was dearly appreciated.

Jeff was the social one; he needed lots of love and his friends. If asked where he was going, it was usually the same smart answer, "I'm going out to keep the streets safe for the little kids." During his adolescence, I once asked him, "Do you know how much I love you?" Rather exasperated, he replied. "Yes, Mom, you tell me a hundred times a day." This was a gross exaggeration on his part, but it was reassuring and let me believe that I was doing something right. Jeff had his own unique way of looking at life. One day, when I was really down on myself, he told me, "Don't be so hard on yourself, Mom. I turned out okay."

Years later, I was asked, "Why do you think your sons turned out okay in spite of all your depressions?" I could think of only one good answer. "They always knew they were loved." They had loving hands to tuck them in each night and frequently heard those life giving words, "I love you." They had the security of a Mom and Dad who cared and were there for them.

As our lives unfolded, there were many good times, many happy times that touched my heart—periods of joy and contentment. There were the everyday happenings like birthdays and sports games, Halloween and Christmas. There were lakes and beaches, camping trips and fishing, cave explorations and the West Edmonton Mall. There were the highlights like Disneyland and the Rocky Mountains, Disneyworld, Niagara Falls, and Canada's Capital. There were graduations and there was leaving home.

The years passed and I was blessed with three wonderful grandchildren. They had the love and support of a loving family to shape and guide them. The boys now are mature, responsible university students. Their sister has already graduated from university and is now pursuing a law degree. She is a beautiful person, inside and out, ready to excel in her world. I thank God every day for them. There were times I cried as I watched them grow, but they were tears of joy because I knew, with certainty, that the cycle of hopelessness and despair, of "nothingness" and "lovelessness" had been broken.

My Husband

To write about my husband is a daunting task, and it might very well sound like one long contradiction.

When I am depressed, I am angry and viciously judgemental, and my husband appears to be unable to say or do anything right, or so it seems to my distorted mind. What I remember most is how involved he was outside the home. Almost every night of the week, there was some activity—some meeting or some sport, or some problem that had to be taken care of. In the early years, it was lacrosse all summer long, some week nights and most weekends. Then the boys were into hockey and they were off with their father to practices and games. At different times throughout the years, their father coached and refereed both lacrosse and hockey and acted as chauffeur and did whatever else was needed. And always there were meetings: the Recreation Board, the Minor Hockey executive, the Separate School Board, and endless hours at different committee meetings. For years, supper had to be ready the minute he walked in the door because it was mostly "eat and run." It's not that I was some sort of slave. It was just that I had a great sense of responsibility and of timing.

He was the husband and father who worked hard and spent whatever hours were necessary to do a good job. He always provided well for his family—paid the bills, did the yard work and maintenance, played with our sons, and went to their games. He loved us. Each Sunday, if he was home, he went to mass with us. Every summer, we went on holidays, carefully calculated to fit his busy schedule. Occasionally, he paid all of us token attention to assuage his guilty conscience, or so it seemed to me.

My husband has always been the perfect example. The husband who never drinks in excess, or even smokes; almost never loses his cool, he rarely shouts, or quarrels. The person who ends anything disagreeable with "I've got a meeting to go to" or "I've got some phone calls to make."

My feelings on this are evident in an excerpt from one of my journals, and as usual, I was depressed as I wrote it. "I could go on ad infinitum, but it really doesn't matter anymore. It will never change; it never has. This is life. And beside I am tired—I can continue in the morning. I should have lots of time. Hockey season's just started, or did it never end? What's important in life? Nothing. What do I want out of life? Nothing. I feel completely defeated. Do I love him? Tomorrow I'll look up the definition of "love," and maybe then I can tell you... But in my heart I know—it always is yes."

It always seemed that my husband was the good guy. I was the one with all the problems; and at times, they were loud and glaring. His absence from home only affected his family, so to the outside world, he appeared flawless.

In the early years especially, I questioned how can someone who's so busy, he's hardly ever home, be fulfilling his obligations as husband and father? How can he be there for so many people but not for his family? Why does it so often feel like he's just passing through, merely a visitor in his own home?

It's not that his family was less important; it was just that his obligations to others were more imperative. If it was a hockey practice or game, or a meeting, and he was involved, he'd be there. Later, any necessary work or phone calls would be looked after. With his family, he could "make it up to them" later, or at least sometimes, in some way.

When our sons were younger, I often felt house bound. There was no time for a movie or dinner out, or time for a game or a puzzle or just being together—no "togetherness"—as in my childhood.

I was told on numerous occasions that my husband was not going to change. When I was feeling good, I, too, accepted that he was not going to change. More importantly, during times like that, I also realized that he didn't need to change; he was a successful functioning adult. I knew deep down inside that I had to change. I would not survive the way I was feeling inside and the way I was living. It hurt too much.

I didn't realize it at the time, but my husband was the strength, the stable support that stood firm and anchored us throughout my many depressive episodes. He was my connection to reality and, ultimately, to survival. When I disappeared within myself, he coped and kept the household going. Life would go on, with all the outward trappings of normality even though, beneath, it was anything but normal. When I felt better, he was there and I'd feel so guilty because I was the one who had been away—sometimes for so long. I shudder to think of what would have happened to me if we had not met, if he had not been so accepting, loving, and steadfast. During the tumultuous times of our marriage, as I sought to find myself, he was my rock, my everyday savior.

I sometimes questioned his understanding, the depth of which became evident to me when he came home from a business trip and handed me two postcards—one was for me, and one was for him. Mine said, "Courage: You must have the courage to be yourself, and not to lose courage for being who you are." And his said "Love: Love me most when I deserve it least; that's when I need it most."

I know, without a doubt, that my husband is an extraordinary person, an honorable person. He has strong Christian values and lives what he believes. In spite of his sports addiction, he's one of the most giving persons I know. Even his sports involvement is in ways that benefits others—those hundreds of girls and boys, and young men whose lives he has touched through the years. He's hardworking to a fault. He's loving and loyal, patient and nonjudgmental. His desire in life is not just to live but "to use himself up." I am proud of him, and I love him dearly.

We have been married for fifty-three years, and the good times have far outweighed the bad. We have reached a stage of joy and contentment, a peace that only God can give. I am now more accepting of his way of life because I have finally found *"me"* and *"mine,"* a new way of living. I feel free to pursue my own interests. I now understand what "live my life" means; it just took me a very long time to get to this point.

My husband's love and loyalty were never shaken irreparably even by my years of mental illness. I know those years will never be completely forgotten but they are past.

There have been many miracles in my life, most of which I didn't recognize at the time. My husband and my two sons were, and still are, the greatest among them.

Treatments and Summation

I have fought the good fight. I have
finished the race. I have kept the faith.
—2 Timothy 4:7

For the most part, through the years, I relied on the help of numerous physicians. With two exceptions, they were less memorable than the ten different psychiatrists I had contact with; some of them just briefly, a consultation or a telepsych conference. With others, the doctor-patient relationship ranged from seven months to nine years. Their care ranged from questionable to negligent, from sarcastic to pompous. There were also those who were patient and caring, compassionate and most helpful. Perhaps I needed all of them to get to where I'm at. But who can justify the years of pain and suffering and how much was unnecessary pain and suffering?

I have been voluntarily hospitalized in the psych ward of four different hospitals. During two of those hospitalizations, I underwent electroconvulsive treatments. I have been prescribed roughly thirty-five to forty different antidepressants, antipsychotics, mood stabilizers, anticonvulsants, stimulants, and tranquilizers. Some of them worked, most of them didn't, and a few sent me on what I call a "bad trip on prescription drugs." I have also been on one experimental drug and through one experimental trial, a specialized formula of multivitamins, minerals, and antioxidants. These didn't help much to alleviate my depressions.

I have undergone extensive psychotherapy and I have been evaluated at St. Michael's Hospital in Toronto and at both the University of Alberta Department of Education and the Lousage Institute. Their conclusions? I am normal.

I was prescribed a Seasonal Affective Disorder light. This light imitates sunlight and is used throughout the winter months to treat S.A.D. caused by our long winters and lack of sunlight this far north. The results were questionable. I experienced little change in mood.

In the latter stages of my recovery, I went through a series of EMDR sessions—As mentioned previously, at first I noticed little change in mindset but gradually, I came to the realization that I could think of my childhood without crying. Was this the result of EMDR or was it the culmination of my lifelong quest for wellness? I can't say.

At present, I am on five different medications. Two are antidepressants, one is an antipsychotic, one an anticonvulsant, and one is a mood stabilizer. I understand that they work together to restore and maintain the balance of neurotransmitters in my brain. This is an over simplification of very complex interactions. This cocktail of medications is especially effective, and it only came about after years of trial and error, so I'm not about to jeopardize what works. It is not the ideal solution I was searching for, but for now, it is working, and I'll take that.

There are those people who would be aghast at the amount of medication I'm on. I call it the high cost of sanity. Let those people take that walk in the shoes of the emergent person and experience the depths of my depressions and feel my tears, then let them make an informed decision. Life is not always fair; it just is. Grudgingly, I've learned to accept this and with acceptance has come a certain amount of peace.

Recently, I was asked who helped me the most during my lengthy illness and recovery. Without hesitation, I replied, "I did. I persevered."

My most excruciating pain, yet my most fulfilling achievement has been giving birth to myself. I am now who I was meant to be.

EPILOGUE

And the end of all our exploring
Will be to arrive where we started
And know the place for the first time
—T.S. Eliot

When I was a teenager, like many people struggling to put a name and meaning to their life journey, I had this burning desire to write a book. It would be called "My Quest for Happiness." I even remember checking the dictionary to assure myself that the word "quest" adequately described what burned within me. Little did I know, at that time, that this longing for happiness is indelibly imprinted within every heart that God creates. But we *cannot* truly partake of this happiness until we come to the realization that it dwells within us and *It* is God.

I do not always feel the presence of God. Mostly, life just goes by, day after day. And sometimes, many, many times, I feel completely lost—abandoned. Still, I know that God is near. He is as near as each breath I breathe.

Throughout my life, in my mind and in my journal writings, one fervent plea has repeated itself. "God, help me to be the person you want me to be." I realize now that, in God's plan, in his eyes, I am that person, and I have always been. This realization was so hard for me to get to. But at mass one day, I was doing a reading from a letter of Paul to the Corinthians. It said, "But by the grace of God I am what I am and his grace toward me has not been in vain." The words caused me to pause because he spoke, as if, from my heart! But by the grace of God, I am what I am. It just took me so long to find myself. And I find myself here exactly where God wants me to be.

I am happy in this place that I'm at. Those tears of mine that sought to express feelings of hurt and pain and despair that lay beyond all speech, have turned into words quite easily spoken. My battle with depression is not over. I now recognize it for what it is, and I'm better equipped to deal with it. I have suffered, but I have learned and I have grown. I am no longer the traumatized, speechless child. I have looked my enemy in the eye and broken free. Depression does not control my life the way it once did. I have found something—*someone*—much more powerful.

I do not know what tomorrow will bring, but I have faith, I hope, and I have love. I believe that this is acceptable to God.

I would like the rest of my life to be a prayer—a prayer of thankfulness that God in his wisdom has molded me to become the person that I am, a prayer of thankfulness for all that I've been given and for what I can give to others.

A famous quotation from Saint Augustine sums up my ongoing quest for happiness most eloquently. "Thou hast made us for thyself, oh God, and our hearts are restless until they rest in Thee."

Peace and God bless.

REFERENCES

Ch. 20 Canadian Mental Health Association Pfizer Can. Inc. 1996, Kirkland, Quebec

Ch. 20 Wina Sturgeon, Prentice Hall, Englewood Cliffs, New Jersey Copyright 1979 Depression, How to Recognize It, How to Cure It, and How to Grow From It

Ch. 21 Ibid.

Ch. 21 Dr. Steven Hyman, Neuroscientist, Provost, Harvard University Childhood abuse leaves chemical "imprint" on brain. Margaret Munro, Canwest News Service (Edmonton Journal, February 2009)

Ch. 34 Charles L Whitfield M.D., Healing the Child Within, Published by Health Communication, Deerfield Beach, Florida 1987, Reprinted 1989 "Afraid of Night", a poem by Ginny pg. 60

Ch. 39 The Collected Works of St. John of the Cross

Ch. 47 EMDR: Unblocking the Mind's Natural Healing Process: An interview with Francine Shapiro, Ph.D. by Sheryll Stuart Thomson M.A., M.F.C.C.

ABOUT THE AUTHOR

Diane Summers, the author of *No Words, Only Tears*, has lived what she writes. She was deeply traumatized by her childhood growing up in poverty and isolation in the back woods of the Ottawa valley. Her earliest memories were those of feeling like a "nothingness" and of belonging nowhere. The loveless, wounded child within her lived on, far into adulthood, as did her feelings of being a "non-person." Throughout her life, depression plagued her. Very early on, she created a false self, a facade behind which to hide to cope with the outside world and her extremely dysfunctional family.

Driven by the desire to change and to escape the pain and chaos of her situation, she was determined to finish high school. She saw education as the foundation upon which to build her future. Due to her perfectionist personality, she sought certainty in all aspects of her life. Faced with the prospect of marriage, she panicked and escaped to a convent for a few years. This was a blessed period of adjustment which she desperately needed before facing the outside world.

There followed marriage and motherhood. In spite of all that her family suffered because of her mental illness, they were a loving and stabilizing force. Like most wives and mothers, she looked after her home and raised two sons.

She spent her years of employment as a bookkeeper and later, she became a volunteer lay counselor. This work was as helpful for her as for her various clients. And still, time and again, she spiraled down to the depths of depression. She felt what it's like to live failure, to battle thoughts of suicide, to wish she were dead.

Armed with sheer determination and dogged perseverance, Diane followed her innate belief that there was a purpose for her existence. She set out to recreate her life from the inside out.

Recovery was an ongoing process and took enormous courage and time. In the face of all her challenges, she found, within herself, untapped strength and resiliency and a deep-rooted will for survival. She went on to prove that old habits can be changed, belief systems can be altered, and a life can be transformed. Finally, she fulfilled her lifelong dream of writing a book. A cathartic exposé of her journey through depression to self-actualization. She lives with her husband in Alberta, Canada.

CPSIA information can be obtained
at www.ICGtesting.com
Printed in the USA
LVHW041416021219
639143LV00001B/4/P

9 781644 926512